To Florence:

Read and enjoy!
All the best!
Shalom,
Art Zannoni

JEWS

&

CHRISTIANS

speak of

JESUS

JEWS & CHRISTIANS

speak of JESUS

ARTHUR E. ZANNONI, *editor*

FORTRESS PRESS   *Minneapolis*

JEWS AND CHRISTIANS SPEAK OF JESUS

Cover design: Brad Norr

Library of Congress Cataloging-in-Publication Data

Jews and Christians speak of Jesus / edited by Arthur E. Zannoni.
    p.   cm.
    Includes bibliographical references (pp. 159–181) and index.
    ISBN 0-8006-2804-7 (alk. paper) :
    1. Jesus Christ—Jewishness. 2. Jesus Christ—Jewish
interpretations. 3. Christianity—Origin. 4. Christianity and
other religions—Judaism. 5. Judaism—Relations—Christianity.
I. Zannoni, Arthur E., 1942–
BT590.J8J48   1994
232.9—dc20   94-18410
                                                      CIP

Manufactured in the U.S.A.   AF 1-2804
98   97   96   95   94   1   2   3   4   5   6   7   8   9   10

CONTENTS

FOREWORD

Established in 1985, the Center for Jewish–Christian Learning at the University of St. Thomas (St. Paul and Minneapolis, Minnesota) has been at the forefront of promoting, publishing, and programming symposia that deal with a variety of issues in the dialogue between Jews and Christians. At no time in the history of the dialogue has there been such a concentrated effort by both religions to build sincere bridges of communication and understanding. In this atmosphere, the center has flourished—on campus, by facilitating various undergraduate courses on Judaism; in its public programming; and in its annually published *Proceedings*. It is accurate to say that the center is known both nationally and internationally for its dedication and commitment to the promotion of serious dialogue and education between Jews and Christians. More than 25,000 persons have attended center-sponsored events since its founding nine years ago. The *Proceedings* is distributed to some 5,000 seminaries, libraries, and individuals annually.

In preparing for our 1993 season, we determined to present a series of symposia under the general title, "Jews and Christians Speak of Jesus." We considered it a bold endeavor and were certain no other institution had attempted such an undertaking. A task force was assembled consisting of Rabbi Barry Cytron, Senior Rabbi, Adath Jeshurun congregation; Dr. Donald Juel, Luther Northwestern Theological Seminary; Dr. John Merkle, College of

Saint Benedict; Rev. Dr. Marilyn Salmon, United Theological Seminary; Karen Schierman, my associate; and Arthur Zannoni, a former associate of the center. I served as convenor. The task force set the agenda, chose the participants, and spent many hours meeting and telephoning to clarify the topics, and then developing with the scholars how each topic would be approached. We decided on four sessions, each addressed by two distinguished scholars—one Jewish, the other Christian. The lectures presented are the context of this volume. A grant from the Jay Phillips Family Foundation was obtained to help defray the cost of the program. Mr. Phillips (1898–1992), a community leader and national philanthropist, was one of the founders of the center and a dear personal friend.

Moreover, we were in contact with Dr. Marshall Johnson of Fortress Press, who submitted to his editorial board a suggestion to consider publishing the lectures as a book, with Arthur E. Zannoni, a member of the task force, as its editor. The board agreed to publish them, and our work on this book began in earnest.

Approximately one thousand persons attended each of the sessions. I found, as I hope readers will, each contributor's essay to be both enlightening and stimulating.

I am most grateful to the eight scholars whose research and reflections appear in this collection. I especially want to thank Fr. Dennis Dease, President of the University of St. Thomas, and Monsignor Terrence J. Murphy, its Chancellor, for their constant support, encouragement, and friendship. Fr. Dease's approval of the program provided us with the impetus we needed to attempt it.

And I am grateful to the members of our task force, who gave so generously of their time and knowledge. Rabbi Cytron, Dr. Juel, Dr. Merkle, and Dr. Salmon each moderated one of our programs, and I thank them for that as well. Finally, I thank my associate, Karen Schierman, who supervised every facet of every program with amazing zest and her usual unbelievable efficiency.

It is my hope that this volume will prove to be not only a contribution to the expanding Jewish–Christian dialogue but also a ready resource for its continuation. May it help us all to grow in knowledge and wisdom, and in respect and concern for one another. May it give us increasing zeal to ensure the religious communities of the world the kind of understanding for which we all pray.

RABBI MAX A. SHAPIRO, Director
Center for Jewish–Christian Learning
University of St. Thomas

INTRODUCTION

The last three decades of the twentieth century have seen, among scholars and the general public, a movement away from monologue and toward dialogue. Ever since the Second Vatican Council (1962–1965), Christians and Jews have attempted to dialogue about each other's faith in the one God. Dialogue groups and interfaith committees are springing up all over the world. Christians are eager to claim their Jewish-faith roots, and Jews want to learn how to live as an authentic and religious minority in a world where there is a Christian majority. As one author stated: "Christianity developed out of a world that was largely Jewish. Jews today live in a world that is deeply influenced by Christianity."

This volume of essays is an example of something new and exciting that is going on in North America, especially between Jews and Christians. For the first time in almost two thousand years, Jews and Christians can sit down as equals around a table and reflect on their profound sameness and deep differences. In a real way, this book represents another step Christians and Jews have taken together on the new road to deeper understanding.

The issues surrounding the Jewish Christian dialogue are legion—the State of Israel, the Holocaust (*Shoah*), and the Jewishness of Jesus, to mention only a few. Dialogue does not mean proselytizing or conversion; instead, each faith tradition recognizes and respects its own identity. Any notion that Christianity has replaced or superseded the Jewish people in God's plan of salvation is both inadmissible and repulsive to the dialogue.

One, if not the central, issue facing serious dialogue between Christians and Jews is Jesus of Nazareth. How can both of these faith communities speak about this itinerant Galilean whose origins and early followers were Jewish and whose subsequent followers broke away from Judaism? This volume attempts to address this question.

The same question is voiced in the Gospel of Mark, where Jesus asks, "Who do people say that I am?" (Mark 8:27). For almost two thousand years, scholars, clergy, and lay people—believers and nonbelievers—have wrestled with the meaning of Jesus. No one has had as profound an influence on Western civilization as he. In fact, the study of the life and time of Jesus has become one of the central factors in current Jewish–Christian dialogue.

Recently, both Jewish and Christian scholarship has emphasized the importance of the world in which Jesus was born and lived. The eight contributors to this volume reflect on and interpret this world. Among the myriad questions raised by their reflections are: Into what kind of a world was Jesus born? What were the social, economic, religious, and political conditions of this world? What were the tensions and antagonisms that resulted from these conditions? Where did he stand in relation to the Judaisms of his time? What are the historical sources of the period? How factual are they? Was Jesus a Pharisee? Did he understand himself to be the "Messiah"? Did he perceive himself as "King of the Jews"? What does the title "Son of man" mean in the light of contemporary sources? Did Jesus intend to found a church? What is the relationship of the church to the synagogue? How did the understanding of the Jesus of history move to the Christ of faith? How did the early church's understanding and teaching move from Christ to God? What does Jesus mean for contemporary Christians and Jews? What new knowledge do the Dead Sea Scrolls bring to our understanding of Jesus? What influence has

Jesus had on Jewish life over the centuries? Can contemporary Jews and Christians better relate to one another through an improved understanding of Jesus' origins as well as of Jesus' interpreters?

To facilitate responses to these questions, the book is divided into four parts. In Part One, "Judaisms at the Time of Jesus," Shaye J. D. Cohen and Anthony J. Saldarini explore the times in which Jesus lived; the social, religious, and economic conditions of the land in which he was born, grew to adulthood, and preached; his relationship to the Judeans of his time; and the forces that shaped his life. The places of the Sadducees, Pharisees, Essenes, the fourth philosophy (the Sicarii), and other minor Jewish sects are addressed and set within the Roman rule of the day.

In Part Two, "The Jewishness of Jesus," Lawrence H. Schiffman and E. P. Sanders reflect on Jesus the Jew and where Jesus stood in relationship to the Judaisms of his time. They are quick to point out that Jesus, in his teaching and style, was akin to the Pharisees. Using the Ten Commandments as a base, these two essayists examine how Jesus lived and worshiped. They explore his convictions pertaining to God and to all humankind, and touch on some of the disagreements between Jesus and other approaches to Jewish life contemporaneous with his own life.

In Part Three, "From Jesus to Christ," Paula Fredriksen presents an encyclopedic overview of how Saul/Paul, the apostle to the Gentiles, contributed to the understanding, interpretation, and teaching that Jesus was the Christ. Her central premise is that Christ, not Jesus, was the heart of Paul's proclamation. Further, she explains how Paul still considered himself a Jew even after his "conversion" to the Jesus movement. In his essay, John R. Donahue, S.J., carefully analyzes the trial of Jesus as narrated in the Gospels of the New Testament and points out the complexities, both historical and theological, surrounding the trial. He also explores the guidelines that should be followed by Christians in assessing Jewish involvement in the death of Jesus.

In Part Four, "From Christ to God," Alan F. Segal and Monika K. Hellwig address how divinity came to be applied to Jesus. In his essay, Segal outlines the factors needed for understanding the movement in interpretation of Jesus from Christ to God. Hellwig details the thinking of the early church fathers and ecumenical councils in their respective approaches to issues surrounding Jesus' divinity, or, better, subsequent faith claims to divinity.

All of the essays represent an ecumenical perspective and are an honest attempt to reflect on the issues surrounding dialogue about Jesus between Jews and Christians. Each essay is affected by the personal experience, scholarship, and religious tradition of the particular author. They all make for fascinating and enlightening reading. To help the reader cull from each essay salient points and key issues, discussion questions have been included at the end of each chapter.

No publication is the product of any one individual. The editor would like to thank all of the contributors for their essays, Rabbi Max A. Shapiro for his encouragement and constant support, Marshall Johnson of Fortress Press for his confidence in my ability, Sue Moro for her computer expertise. Special appreciation is extended to Karen Schierman of the Center for Jewish–Christian Learning, at the University of St. Thomas, whose countless hours of dedicated and meticulous work on the manuscript paved the way for its publication. Finally, I would like to thank my spouse, Kathleen Flannery Zannoni, consummate person, whose companionship graces my life and whose spirit lights up the dark spaces.

It is hoped that this volume will prove to be a stimulus to the continuing dialogue between Jews and Christians and a witness to the world of "How very good and pleasant it is when kindred live together in unity!" (Ps 132:1).

Arthur E. Zannoni

PART ONE

JUDAISMS AT THE TIME OF JESUS

1

JUDAISM AT THE TIME OF JESUS

SHAYE J. D. COHEN

◼

I would like to remind us all that this week is Holocaust Awareness Week, in which we mark Yom Hashoah and the fiftieth anniversary of the uprising of the Warsaw Ghetto (September 1943). This fact is not irrelevant in this context. I think that what we are doing here at the University of St. Thomas represents one of the wonderful fruits of living in our country. We are engaged in an open and frank dialogue between Jews and Christians, between Judaism and Christianity. In contrast, in pre-Holocaust Europe, Judaism never entered university curricula, and ecumenical dialogue did not exist. This was a great tragedy. Abraham Joshua Heschel, speaking of Jewish life in Warsaw in the 1930s, said, "We knew we were doomed, but we had nobody to talk to." I hope that none of us is doomed in the same way that he and his world were doomed, but at least we will have somebody to talk to.

The issue before us is unity versus diversity, or Judaism versus Judaisms.[1] Let me begin with a brief introduction.

What do we mean by Judaism? For most people, Judaism is a "religion." This definition may or may not be correct for contemporary culture, but I don't think it is correct for antiquity. As soon as

3

we use the word "religion," we are immediately thrusting on antiquity a category or set of categories that is not entirely appropriate or that is as misleading as it is helpful. Judaism was not a "religion" in antiquity; Judaism became a "religion" only in the nineteenth century. As Jews left the ghetto, became emancipated, and joined the new nation-states of nineteenth-century Europe, their Jewishness had to be "compartmentalized" and separated from other aspects of their identity. The Jews became, or attempted to become, citizens of France, Germany, England, Italy, and so on—like all other citizens except that their religion was Judaism. In the course of the nineteenth century, Judaism (that is, the Jewish religion) became only one aspect of "Jewishness"; many Jews abandoned their religion but expressed their Jewishness through language, literature, art, culture, politics, and in other ways. In premodern times, however, Judaism had not yet been formalized as a religion. It was the way of life of the Jews. All the things about the Jews that made them "peculiar," different, special—in short, that made them *Jews*—all together, these characteristics, traits, practices, ideas, attitudes, and rituals constituted what the ancients called *Ioudaismos*, Judaism. Similarly, all the things that collectively made Greeks Greeks were called *Hellenismos*, Hellenism. Hellenism was not a religion, but the way of life of the Greeks. Judaism is not (just) a religion, but the way of life or culture or civilization of the Jews.

Who are these Jews (in Greek, *Ioudaioi*) of whom we are speaking? There are three overlapping answers: (1) geographical, (2) ethnic, and (3) cultural. First is the geographical answer: Jews were the inhabitants of Judea (whom, in English, we might call "Judeans"). Judea, in turn, can be defined either narrowly, so that it refers to the district around Jerusalem, the ancient portion of the tribe of Judah, or broadly, so that it refers to the entire area, including the districts of Galilee, Transjordan, the coastal plain, Samaria, Judea, and Idumea. Second is the ethnic answer: Jews are members of an ethnic group bound together by (a myth of) common ancestry. By the first century of our era, memories of tribal affiliation had all but died out (except in the memories and imaginations of princes and visionaries), but most Jews thought of themselves as descendants of the tribe of Judah, one of the twelve sons of Jacob. Politically speaking, the Jews of Judea were regarded by their neighbors and conquerors as an *ethnos*, a nation, whose defining element in antiquity (and in modern times) was common descent from a single group of progenitors. Third is the cultural answer: Jews are those, whether living in Judea or outside of it, whether descendants of the tribe of Judah or not, who identify themselves, or are identified by others, as Jews and who practice or hope to practice a Jewish way of life. In antiquity, Jews were scattered throughout the entire eastern Mediterranean basin: Italy, Greece, modern-day Turkey (ancient Asia Minor), Syria, Judea, Egypt and north Africa, and modern-day Libya (ancient Cyrenaica). All these areas had large numbers of Jews in a variety of communities. These three answers often overlap, but occasionally the distinctions among them are important. Thus, diaspora Jews are Jews only in the sense of answers (2) and (3); they are not Judeans. Converts to Judaism are Jews only in the sense of answer (3). In this brief essay, I cannot pursue these distinctions and their ramifications, and so I shall use "Jews" mostly in the third sense.

Modern scholars correctly observe that it is impossible to imagine that, in the first century of the Common Era, all the Jews of all these far-flung places followed a uniform way of life. There was no single political structure that included all these people called Jews. They did not belong to a single organization, and no governmental body, whether Jewish or Roman, exercised jurisdiction over all of them insofar as they were Jews. The Jews of Alexandria were governed in one way, the Jews of Antioch in another, the Jews of Judea in a third, and so on. And, most important to emphasize: there was no pope. The closest ancient Jewish analog to a pope would have been the high priest of the Temple of Jerusalem, a figure well-known to us all from the gospel accounts of the trial of Jesus. The high priest had not the authority, and certainly not the power, to protect the faith of the faithful, distinguish "orthodox" from "heretical" Judaism, or define who was and who was not in communion with some equivalent of holy mother church. This was not his function. He did exercise some measure of influence on the politics of Judea, but his chief responsibility was to take care of the temple, keep rabble-rousers out of the way, and, if they made too much noise and caused trouble, hand them over to the Romans to be taken care of properly.

Scholars sometimes ascribe to the high priest—and, later, to the leader of the rabbinic movement, the *patriarch*—powers and influence that even a modern pope, let alone a chief rabbi, would envy, as if the high priest would regularly send out messengers to the communities of the Diaspora, as if these messengers somehow had the authority to enforce doctrinal and ritual "orthodoxy," and as if all Jews had to yield to the authority of these messengers. All this is fantasy. Its roots lie in the early Christian traditions about the emissaries sent out by the high priest of Jerusalem to make sure that Jews throughout the Roman Empire were expelling and anathematizing Christians.

There was no central Jewish political organization. There was no pope. Furthermore, Jews spoke many different languages. In Judea, as far as we can tell, learned Jews may have spoken Hebrew, others probably spoke Aramaic, some spoke Greek. The Jews of the Diaspora certainly spoke Greek and probably next to no Hebrew. In Judea, there would have been people who conversed in Aramaic, prayed in Hebrew, and knew enough Greek to speak to soldiers and government officials. In the Diaspora, Jews did all this communicating in Greek. How could they have shared sacred texts with their Judean brethren? How could they have discussed theology, law, ritual, even politics? These facts, coupled with the wide variety of: literature and documentation extant from the Second Temple period (retellings of the Bible, commentaries on the Bible, replacements of the Bible, apocalypses, testaments, wisdom literature, oracles, psalms, hymns, prayers, polemics, apologetics, histories, whether written in Greek, Hebrew, or Aramaic, in some cases reflecting sectarian or pietistic perspectives); social types and groups that influenced Jewish opinion and behavior (holy men, prophets, miracle workers, scribes, elders, priests, high priests, messiahs, brigands, teachers, revolutionaries, the well-to-do, aristocrats); social settings in which Jews lived (cities and rural villages, some predominantly Jewish and others predominantly gentile, in Judea and in the Diaspora); and diverse political opinions among the Jews (rebels with various beliefs, partisans of peace and various levels of appeasement; advocates and opponents of cooperation with Gentiles), lead to the conclusion that the ways of life of all these Jews scattered throughout the Mediterranean world were so diverse, so multiformed, so inconsistent, and so impossible to conceive in monistic terms, that we must speak not only of "varieties" of Judaism but even, as some scholars have contended, of Judaisms (plural).

All these facts are true, but we should not allow our modern obsession with diversity and pluralism to blind us to another set of facts. Not a single ancient author, whether Jewish or non-Jewish, said that the Jews of antiquity were so divided among themselves that they followed diverse Judaisms or systems. Some authors (notably Juvenal and Tacitus) saw the Jews as a vaguely sinister group, united in their goal of subverting the Roman state and Roman values (a version of the "Jewish conspiracy" theory). It is well known that where insiders see strife and discord, outsiders see harmony and agreement. Insiders tend to dwell on and magnify in-group differentia; outsiders tend to lump "the other" together in a single undifferentiated group. The failure of Greek and Roman writers to comment on Jewish diversity might be considered a function of their perspective as outsiders, were not the same point made by an insider. In *Against Apion*, Josephus writes as follows:

> Unity and identity of religious belief, perfect uniformity in habits and customs, produce a very beautiful concord in human character. Among us alone will be heard no contradictory statements about God such as are common among other nations, not only on the lips of ordinary individuals under the impulse of some passing mood, but even boldly propounded by philosophers; some putting forward crushing arguments against the very existence of God, others depriving him of his providential care for mankind. Among us alone will be seen no difference in the conduct of our lives. With us all act alike, all profess the same doctrine about God, one which is in harmony with our law and affirms that all things are under his eye. Even our womenfolk and dependents will tell you that piety must be the motive of all our occupations in life. (*Ag. Ap.* 2.19.179–81)

In this treatise, Josephus returns to this theme several times, even remarking that Jews are admired by Gentiles for their concord (*Ag. Ap.* 1.39.283). These passages are somewhat troubling in view of the fact that Josephus elsewhere tells us about the Pharisees, the Sadducees, and the Essenes, not to mention the Samaritans, the "fourth philosophy" (apparently the Sicarii), the Zealots, and the tribe of people who follow Jesus called the Christ. Josephus himself describes all these groups, but this fact does not prevent him from praising the uniformity and unanimity of the Jews in matters relating to God.

No matter how this contradiction is to be explained, Josephus emphasizes that all Jews, even womenfolk and children, know the law and agree on what the law is. Here, then, is praise for Jewish uniformity and harmony. No ancient document claims, as modern scholars regularly do, that Judaism is a diverse phenomenon consisting of conflicting and inconsistent sets of systems.

In the ancient world, outsiders had no doubt what Judaism was. Greek and Roman writers who talked about Jews and Judaism

8

knew exactly what Judaism was all about. Judaism was the way of life of the Jews. What struck outsiders about that way of life were three things you and I might call "religious": (1) the Sabbath (Jews do not work on the Sabbath); (2) circumcision (Jewish men are circumcised); and (3) the kosher food laws (Jews' abstinence from pork, for example). If any ancient writer said anything about Jews and Judaism, it probably was a reference to one of these three practices. In fourth place was the Jewish avoidance of images: the Jewish God was not worshiped through images. Not a single ancient author said that some Jews follow these practices while others do not. The Qumran scrolls, the books of the Apocrypha and Pseudepigrapha, the New Testament, and rabbinic literature reveal that the Jews of antiquity debated at great length the precise meaning of all four of these requirements. What kinds of work are prohibited on the Sabbath (for example, may I rescue an animal that has fallen into a pit or may I heal on the Sabbath)? What is the meaning of circumcision, and why is it so important (can Gentiles find favor in God's eyes even without circumcision)? Why should we abstain from certain foods (do the prohibited foods represent certain negative or reprehensible qualities we are to avoid)? How consistent and rigorous must we be in our avoidance of graven images? From antiquity until now, Jews have argued about these questions. But these debates did (and do) not change the truth of the fundamental perception held by outsiders: these practices are somehow uniformly characteristic of "the Jews," no matter whether we are speaking of the Jews of Rome, Alexandria, or Judea.

In fact, a whole series of institutions and ideas served to unify the scattered Jewish communities. I will list (some of) these very briefly. First was the temple in Jerusalem, the most obvious unifying force in ancient Judaism and the focal point of Jewish piety. Many Jews went on pilgrimage to the temple and contributed a half-shekel annually. Sectarians or pietists may have attacked the temple, claiming that the priesthood was corrupt and the sacrifices were not being done properly (see, for example, the story of Jesus cleansing the temple, Matt 21:12-13, an act of a militant Jewish pietist in preparation for some new, better, and purer temple to replace the corrupt one in the end time), but this fact only serves to emphasize the temple's centrality and defining character. When Emperor Caligula announced his intention to place a statute of himself in the temple, tens of thousands of Jews rushed to its defense, threatening not rebellion but mass martyrdom: they would sooner see themselves killed than see the temple defiled. For many Jews, the temple was the footstool of the divine throne, the palace of God, and the one place where heaven and earth meet. The sacrificial cult of the temple protected the natural order, guaranteeing plentiful rain and abundant harvests, warding off disaster and disease. The temple was the center of the Jewish world.

The second unifying force was "the book," the Torah, sometimes called "the Law." The Torah (made up of the biblical books of Genesis, Exodus, Leviticus, Numbers, and Deuteronomy) was not an esoteric book or the possession of a small coterie of priests, like the sacred books of the Egyptians, Phoenicians, and many other peoples. It was a public book, the possession of all, and it united the public of its readers. It belonged to the community and was studied communally every week in the synagogue, "the assembly." Jews revered it and lived their lives by it. The Jews disagreed among themselves about the correct interpretation of this book and the identity of those authorized to interpret it, but these disagreements did not detract from its centrality and unifying character. The Torah became a symbol as well as a book. When a revolutionary leader wanted to stir up his followers, he could hold the Torah scroll aloft and proclaim, "This is what you are fighting for!" Gentiles knew that Moses, the lawgiver of the Jews, had given his laws in a book that was the determinant of Jewish law.

As the third unifying force, we can point to a single dominant Jewish theology. E. P. Sanders of Duke University calls it "covenantal nomism," a fancy term for the rather obvious fact that Jews believe "the book" comes from God and contains a covenant, a contract. Jews and God are bound to each other through the terms of this covenant; the Jews are obligated to observe "the Law" in return for being God's people. This basic theology (with numerous variations, of course) characterized virtually all forms of Judaism known to us from antiquity.

The fourth unifying force, a belief in one chief God, was shared by all Jews in antiquity. The Jews argued among themselves about the number and efficacy of angels, demons, spirits, and other intermediaries; about the mysterious ways of God's providence and the origins of evil; about the existence and reality of the gods of other nations; and about much else. But none of these debates and disputes detracts from the fundamental theological unity that was shared by all forms of Judaism known to us from antiquity.

Finally, in my view, all Jews of antiquity were animated by some sense of separation or differentness. The Jews argued among themselves about the degree of separation that must be observed. Some Jews advocated a strict separation from the Gentiles, regarding their wine, oil, cheese, and milk—and, especially, their daughters—as impure. Other Jews had a more open, accommodating, and realistic attitude toward the outside world. But even these latter Jews, often the most enlightened, well-educated, Hellenized Jews, realized that their Jewishness made them different from the world around them. Philo, for example, the very model of a Hellenized Jew, in one passage reveals that he saw the world in terms of "us" over against "them." A certain self-consciousness caused Jews to separate themselves from the world, at least to some degree. "Apostate" Jews tried to efface this distinction, but the bulk of Jews accepted it.

I conclude from this brief survey that, for all of its varieties and plurality, debates and disputes, schools and sects, there was a Judaism in antiquity, a set of beliefs, practices, and institutions shared by the overwhelming majority of people calling themselves Jews and being so identified by others. This thesis is born not of religious fundamentalism or historical naïveté, but of an effort to see unity without denying diversity.

For Discussion

1. What is meant by Judaism in antiquity? Was it a "religion" or a way of life?

2. Why are there geographical, ethnic, and cultural answers to the question, Who were the Jews of antiquity?

3. Was there just one Judaism or a variety of Judaisms in antiquity?

4. What were the three practices of Judaism that "outsiders" (non-Jews) saw as unique to a Jewish way of life?

5. What were the various unifying forces in the scattered Jewish communities of antiquity?

6. From reading this chapter, what new insights have you gained about the Jews of antiquity?

2

PLURALISM OF PRACTICE
AND BELIEF IN
FIRST-CENTURY JUDAISM

ANTHONY J. SALDARINI

■

When we Jews and Christians look at ourselves today, each community thinks of itself as one and as different from the other. But when
we look hard at ourselves or one another, the lines that separate and
unite are not so sharp, clear, and uncrossable. Liberal, educated
American Jews and Christians have more in common with each
other in many ways, even religiously, than American Jews have with
Israeli *haredim* or Ethiopian Jews or than American urban Christians have with Christian farmers in Madras, South India, or Christian fishermen on the islands in the Amazon delta. Within any
religious tradition, groups separated by space, time, language, culture, and history differ greatly from one another even as they share
core values and symbols. One further complication: In the first
century, Christianity had not established itself as a separate religion
and community. Many followers of Jesus were Jews and identified

13

themselves as such. If you asked Paul what he was, he would say a Jew. What else could he answer? He does not use the word Christian.

GEOGRAPHICAL DIVERSITY OF JEWISH COMMUNITIES

Then, as now, Jews and Christians lived according to local culture and custom. All Jews in the first century acknowledged the temple in Jerusalem as the central and unique shrine of Israel, but most were far removed from the temple and saw it seldom, if ever. Jews dispersed throughout the Roman and Parthian empires might journey to Jerusalem once in their lives, but they lived according to local Jewish customs under the direction of indigenous community officials. The chief priests and other authorities in Jerusalem could exercise no direct authority over the hundreds of local communities of Jews. Their influence on Jews as near as Galilee was limited, because Galilee was ruled by its own tetrarch, Herod Antipas, son of Herod the Great. Galilean cities, towns, and villages had rulers and elders who were independent of the priests and elders in Jerusalem.[1] Talmudic Judaism, with its rabbis, which developed during the second to sixth centuries and ruled most medieval Jewish communities in the Middle East and Europe, did not yet exist.[2] Granted a number of generally accepted texts, norms, and practices, local practice in all its variety was the norm. This is as true today as it was then.

The imperial government and traditional local authorities are the most obvious and neglected leadership groups in the study of ancient Judaism and Christianity. In the first century, the Roman imperial authorities gave local communities, in the persons of their village elders or recognized officials, the authority to administer internal communal affairs and to punish lawbreakers through fines and physical punishments. In the Diaspora, the Jewish communities in cities were often recognized as political entities with their own quarter of the city and their own officials responsible for public order and tax collection. Jews often organized assemblies (in Greek, "synagogues") in which they prayed on Sabbath and received education in Jewish tradition, and through which they functioned as a public body in the larger Greco-Roman world.[3]

Jews had spread all over the Mediterranean region and Mesopotamia (contemporary Iraq) in many roles. Jewish communities in Mesopotamia flourished for more than fifteen hundred years. Under the Persian Empire, Jewish mercenaries were stationed at Elephantine in upper Egypt, where they had their own brand of worship of Yahu.[4] Jews were sent to Asia Minor to found a military colony under the Greek Seleucids. In Alexandria, the cultural capital of Hellenistic civilization, Jews were a numerous, educated, and powerful minority. In Rome, several synagogues with a less numerous and less learned membership flourished, despite occasional trouble with the authorities.[5] In Asia Minor and Greece, many cities had groups of Jews who were farmers, artisans, merchants, and soldiers. Inscriptions tell us that some Jews were wealthy but many were not. In the Roman Empire, Jews were a numerous, vital, recognized, ancient ethnic–religious community with legal privileges and duties, despite occasional persecution. Jewish communities, like other groups, varied greatly in composition, status, and ethos.

THE SOCIAL COMPLEXITY OF GALILEE

Let us take a closer look at Galilee, a region in Israel where Jews lived peacefully and prosperously, so that we can understand its geography, politics, economics, social structure, and culture. Life involved a complex set of relationships and interactions with the empire, local society, the international and local economy, and ancient tradition. Galilee, the northern region of Israel, is divided into a northern, mountainous part called Upper Galilee and the southern Esdraelon or Jezreel Valley, called Lower Galilee.[6] We shall concentrate on

15

Lower Galilee, because we can know more about Jewish life there and also because a local, popular preacher came from a village, Nazareth, situated on a slope in the central part of the Esdraelon and did much of his teaching in the northeastern corner of the valley, on the shore of the Sea of Galilee, near Capernaum (Mark 2:1; Matt 9:1).

Life in Galilee centered on agriculture and fishing. Galilee was densely settled, with small farming villages and hamlets every mile or two, surrounded by fertile fields. The valley that made up most of Lower Galilee was relatively small, only twenty-five miles west to east from the Mediterranean to the Sea of Galilee and fifteen miles south to north from the mountains of Samaria to the mountains of Upper Galilee. Its small size is crucial. Lower Galilee was the size of a modern metropolitan area. One can walk from the Sea of Galilee to the Mediterranean in one long, hot day. To visualize Galilee in terms of the Gospels, the people who came to hear Jesus did not travel far and, in most cases, could walk home in the evening.

Probably only a small percentage of the population was literate and had immediate interests beyond the village or town. However, Galilee was not a rural backwater, unaffected by Greco-Roman culture. The Esdraelon Valley was a major trade route. It offered a level passage through the mountains that separated the coast of the Mediterranean Sea from inland Syria and the caravan routes to Damascus and Mesopotamia. The modern road north of Nazareth, visible from the mound of Sepphoris, running through the Beth Netofa Valley, is the old caravan route. Galilee exported wine and olive oil to other parts of the empire and imported luxury goods for the rich and other fine wares.

Galilee had two large cities, Sepphoris and Tiberias (20,000 inhabitants?), and several smaller ones, such as Bethsaida and Capernaum (10,000?). The cities were closely linked, economically and socially, to the villages and countryside.[7] Sepphoris was only three miles north of Nazareth, so presumably Jesus was familiar with it, even though it is never mentioned in any gospel traditions. The city had been destroyed when it revolted against the Romans after Herod's death (4 B.C.E.). Herod Antipas, ruler of Galilee and son of Herod the Great, rebuilt Sepphoris as the capital of Galilee and a major fortress in the early first century C.E., when Jesus was growing up. Its new population was probably a mixture of Jews and non-Jews involved with the government and commerce. Numerous pools that may have been ritual baths have been found, but so have mosaics and a theater, built during the first century. In the revolt against Rome (66 C.E.), Sepphoris remained loyal to Rome and survived the war.[8] Tiberias, on the west coast of the Sea of Galilee, was built by Herod Antipas as a new capital for himself. Antipas settled it with foreigners and landless poor. Its mixed population, its site on a graveyard, and its Hellenistic public buildings, complete with images, made it offensive to many Jews.

Herod Antipas ruled Galilee and Perea, across the Jordan, for the Romans from 4 B.C.E. until he was removed from office under suspicion of sedition in 39 C.E. As a member of the imperial governing class, he traveled frequently, maintained complex personal and political relations with the emperors and their court, and lived a life far removed from that of the ordinary farmer. Antipas, who is mentioned a number of times in the Gospels and Acts, was a typical native ruler, accommodating himself to Roman customs and practices outside his own country and for the most part fulfilling his obligations toward Judaism at home. He engaged in large building projects and cultivated patrons in Rome. He divorced his wife and married his niece with the ease of an upper-class Roman. As the ruler responsible for keeping the peace, he was apprehensive about the growing reputation of Jesus, as he had been about John the Baptist whom he executed for criticizing his biblically illicit marriage (Mark 6:14; Luke 13:31; cf. also 23:7-12). The Herodians mentioned in the Gospels (Mark 3:6; 12:13) were the officials and upper-class supporters of Herod Antipas who sought to blunt the influence of Jesus whom they saw as a dangerous new political force and a threat to their control.

In the villages and small cities, people came into contact with a number of lower-level officials. For example, according to the Gospels, Jesus came into contact and conflict with lower-level imperial and local community officials. The centurions who appear from time to time were Roman officials stationed at key points such as Capernaum (Mark 5:22). The Pharisees and scribes, who are mentioned often in the Gospels, were probably subordinate officials and functionaries of either Herod Antipas or the Jerusalem authorities. Jairus, the ruler of the synagogue (Mark 5:22), was a prominent local leader. When Josephus, the aristocratic Jerusalem priest, went to Galilee at the beginning of the war with Rome to organize resistance, he came into contact and conflict with village and city elders and ambitious members of the wealthier families. Lower-level officials were subordinate to the small percentage of the wealthy families who exercised direct power; yet they, along with the wealthy and powerful, were separated from the majority of the population, who were farmers, artisans, or landless. The governing classes were generally literate, had access to tax revenues to support themselves, and were not compelled to put most of their efforts into manual labor. Consequently, they formed an independent social network far removed by fixed social position and wealth from that of the village and town.[9]

As in all ancient society, about 90 percent of the people were farmers who lived in small towns or villages and walked out to their fields daily. Because the Esdraelon Valley was fertile, the farmers there were reasonably prosperous. However, prosperity for ancient farmers meant subsistence living with no opportunity for most to improve their station or build up a reserve for times of want. The government, which collected taxes from the small landholder, or the landlord, who collected rent and paid the government in turn (anywhere from 30 percent to 70 percent of the crop), had the small farmers under their control. Farmers often fell into debt in bad years when they borrowed money to pay their taxes and rent; a series of bad years could lead to loss of land or tenancy and thus landlessness.[10] (Joseph was a landless artisan, so Jesus' family had experienced this process at some point.)

Galilee, like other parts of the Middle East, had known invasion and war from time to time. The Romans conquered Galilee in the sixties and fifties B.C.E. and reorganized its governance into new districts to break the power of the traditional leaders. The Parthians invaded the eastern part of the Roman Empire, including Israel, in 40 B.C.E. and installed the Hasmonean Aristobulus II in place of his brother Hyrcanus as high priest and ruler. Three years later, the Romans drove the Parthians back and installed Herod the Great as a client king. To secure his kingdom, Herod did battle with Galilean bandits or brigands, that is, landless and homeless families who lived in caves and unsettled parts of the hills and supported themselves by stealing from the rich. Historical accounts from this period testify to a succession of disorders and revolutionary leaders who protested governmental and economic conditions and sought to reestablish a more just Jewish commonwealth under God.[11] On the other hand, most of the people lived quietly and went about their business, hoping to be spared the sufferings of want and war. Against the background of the majority of the people, who lived life according to local customs and cultural traditions, let us look at some of the specialized social groups of the first century.

REFORMIST MOVEMENTS

In the land of Israel, a number of social movements with religious and political agendas and goals arose during the Greco-Roman period. From the Maccabean persecution on (mid-second century B.C.E.), various groups hoped for divine intervention to free Israel from foreign rule and oppression. Many were apocalyptic movements, typified by the visions in the book of Daniel. They awaited the direct intervention of God to sweep away the evil powers. Using mythic, historical, and prophetic traditions from the Bible, various authors reported visions of the heavenly world and future judgment of the wicked as protests against the political oppression of Israel by world empires and the corruption of Israel's leadership. Apocalyptic imagery, the emerging belief in life after death, and traditional eschatological confidence in the triumph of God's justice reaffirmed the reality of the heavenly world. In the face of overwhelming oppression, apocalypses encouraged confidence in God's power and justice.[12]

In most apocalypses, a human holy man is instructed by a vision, message, or heavenly journey mediated or interpreted by an angel. The content of the message concerns the history of good and evil, the events of the end time, and the ultimate destiny of humanity. Equally important are descriptions of the heavens and hell, various types of angels, and the workings of the cosmos, stars, and weather.[13] All these future events, heavenly places, fantastic figures, and even esoteric knowledge of the universe engendered confidence in the larger divine universe within which the immediately perceptible world is set. It especially promoted confidence in the divine will to enforce justice on behalf of the faithful.

The writing of apocalypses and use of apocalyptic imagery were not limited to specialized groups but were broadly distributed within Jewish society. This stream of Jewish hope and religious expression influenced the Essenes, Pharisees, Jesus, and some of the revolutionaries in the first century. All shared a dissatisfaction with the political, social, religious, and economic life in the land and blamed society's leaders, domestic and foreign, for the state of affairs. All looked for thorough reform and for the ultimate intervention of God. For some groups, apocalyptic thought was central; for others, it was subordinate to other intellectual and social interests. We lack the names of the groups that produced many of the documents that have survived. For example, the Ethiopic Book of Enoch (1 Enoch) contains a dream vision, often referred to as the "Animal Apocalypse" (chs. 85–90), which reviews biblical history through the Maccabean War against the Seleucids in the second century B.C.E.[14] The author is strongly critical of the "shepherds," that is, Jewish leaders previous to the Maccabees, and the gentile imperial authorities. He puts his hope in the awakening of lambs who began to open their eyes (ch. 90), presumably his group or movement, and the great horn that grew on one of the sheep (Judas Maccabee). Although the author's evaluation of Jewish history and unfaithfulness is clear, his group or movement has no name and is difficult to describe in any detail. Similarly, in the first century B.C.E., some group(s) produced the Psalms of Solomon as a protest against the final Hasmonean rulers and the Roman conquest of Jerusalem in 63 B.C.E. The author(s)' views of social conflict is clear, but the name and nature of the group are not.

Thanks to Josephus, Philo, the Dead Sea Scrolls, the New Testament, and Pliny, we know the names of some Jewish groups of the Second Temple period, especially the Essenes, Pharisees, Sadducees, "Fourth (revolutionary) Philosophy" of Judas and Zadok, and the inhabitants of Qumran (most probably a type of Essene). We also know of the followers of various teachers and reformers such as John the Baptist, Jesus, and Bannus; revolutionaries who gathered followings and claimed to be prophets or kings, such as Athronges and Simon; bandit leaders such as the Galileans Ezekias and his son Judas; and, finally, the coalition of forces called the Zealots and the Sicarii at the time of the war against Rome, along with various factional leaders such as Jesus the Galilean, John of Gischala, Simon bar Giora, and Eleazar ben Simon. Today, we might classify some of these figures as political leaders; in the first century, political, social, and religious positions and movements were intertwined as an integral whole. After a brief review of this variety of groups, movements, and leaders, we shall classify them sociologically and evaluate their roles in and contributions to Jewish society as a whole.

The Essenes, especially the branch that had its center at Qumran near the Dead Sea, were in conflict with the chief priests and governmental administration in Jerusalem over the nature of Israel and its role in the world.[15] They considered the worship conducted at the temple to be defective because the high priest was not from the proper family and the ritual was not conducted with adequate purity according to correct rules. The compromises made by the Maccabees with the Seleucid kings in Syria in order to attain relative autonomy for the nation went too far for the Essenes. The infiltration of Hellenistic modes of social organization and cultural expression into the Jewish community was contrary to the strict adherence to biblical law advocated in Essene teachings. Thus, a renewal of the covenant was needed. Devotion to prayer and study of Scripture, meals eaten in careful ritual purity, deep respect for elders and priests as leaders and teachers, and charitable attention to all members of the community marked the rules followed at Qumran. This way of life stressed peace and charity within the community and the avoidance of all conflict and impropriety. The Essenes' ideal contrasted sharply with the changeable and often brutal world of Hellenistic politics in Jerusalem. Wars of succession and civil unrest racked Israel during the last two centuries B.C.E. At Qumran, the Essenes awaited the coming of the Lord with his angels to destroy the human and demonic agents of evil and reestablish a pure temple and a just society. To prepare for these cosmic events, the sectarians at Qumran devoted their whole lives to the service of God according to their unique understanding of the Bible and divine will. These Essenes fit our idea of a withdrawn sect, a group that goes apart from the world to make its own ideal world. Many Essenes, however, lived in cities and towns and were more active politically in the conflicts that marked the Hasmonean and Herodian periods. Essenes noted for their integrity, holiness, and ability to foretell the future appear occasionally in Second Temple period history.

Most Jewish sects and social movements did not withdraw from society as the Qumran group did. The Pharisees began as a religious, social movement in the mid-second century B.C.E., after the Hasmoneans gained power. They sought to reform Jewish society by bringing it into closer conformity with biblical law as they interpreted it. Because their religious views about Judaism necessarily had political and social consequences and implications, they were a political interest group. They sought to influence the governing class and ultimately triumph in a quest for direct power over social laws and policies.[16] Under John Hyrcanus (134–104 B.C.E.), they originally had great influence on how the law was enforced, but a dispute with a Sadducean court rival led to loss of influence and the ascendancy of Sadducean laws and customs in the royal court. Under Alexander Jannaeus, noted for his many wars and the turbulence of his reign (103–76 B.C.E), the Pharisees led the opposition and many suffered persecution and death. Alexander was unpopular, so the Pharisees gained influence with the people. In order to secure her own position as ruler, Alexandra, the wife and successor of Alexander, made an alliance with the Pharisees in which they were given direct power over domestic policy. The Pharisees imposed their laws on society and punished their enemies among the officials of the former king, Alexander. After Alexandra's death, they lost influence and their power was broken. Throughout the rest of the first century B.C.E. and the first century C.E., the Pharisees strove continually to promote their policies. They sought unsuccessfully to influence the succession after Herod died (4 B.C.E.). A prominent and wealthy Pharisee, Simeon, and the notables of the Pharisees appear among the aristocratic leaders in Jerusalem who attempted to avoid war against Rome (66–70 C.E.). The Pharisees' conflicts with Jesus of Nazareth and his followers can be explained as part of their long-term program to influence and reform Jewish society and to oppose those who had different understandings of God's will for Israel.

The Pharisees sought to sanctify Israel, both the land and people, and thus to increase Israel's union with God in a time of great political and cultural challenge. They supported the temple worship by insisting on a careful observance of the laws of tithing, and they extended the sanctity of the temple and its priesthood to the people and daily life by observing biblical rules of ritual purity at home. Food was to be prepared and eaten in ritual purity and kept apart from all untithed and impure food. Sabbath was rigorously observed, and the laws and traditions of Israel were lovingly studied and interpreted.[17] The Pharisees' demand for an intense level of commitment appealed to many who sought a way of adhering to Israel's traditions in new circumstances.

Like the Pharisees, the Sadducees were a reform group, although their program is less well understood than those of the Essenes and Pharisees.[18] Sadducees were drawn from the chief priests and wealthy leaders of society, but not all nor even a majority belonged to the Sadducees. They adhered to the traditional interpretation of the Bible, which means that they rejected the new beliefs in an apocalyptic end of the world and in some form of afterlife, such as resurrection and immortality of the soul, and would not adopt many of the customs and interpretations of biblical law proposed by the Pharisees. When the Mishnah and Tosefta, the earliest rabbinic documents, contrast the Pharisees and Sadducees, disputes over ritual purity laws and practices predominate. Josephus says that they were disliked by the people because they were stern and rigorous in their interpretations of the law. Using Hellenistic categories, Josephus also says that the Sadducees rejected fate and stressed human responsibility. He is probably referring to their rejection of an apocalyptic divine intervention in human affairs.

The mélange of views attributed to the Sadducees is typical of the governing classes' holding on to their superior position in society. The Sadducees stressed this world (in which they ruled) rather than a coming, ideal world. They saw God at work in biblically established institutions, such as the temple, which were controlled by them. They emphasized human free will and responsibility because they had control over the government in Jerusalem and, thus, an opportunity to influence society. They rejected new customs and understandings of the Bible and Jewish life because such innovations threatened their position in society. They fought for their ways of observing purity regulations and administering justice because they were allied with the social class that ruled the temple and the courts. The Sadducees themselves were not coextensive with the governing class and priesthood. They were a minority reform group with an agenda aimed at the whole governing class and, ultimately, at society at large. It is likely that their stress on Israel's traditions was a reaction against overhellenization by some of the ruling families and officials and an evidence of the Sadducees' desire to preserve the earlier way of living Judaism.

Some reformers were popular teachers and preachers who exhorted and warned the people to repent, renew the covenant, obey God's commands, and turn Israel into what it should be in God's eyes. John the Baptist, whose austere life and fatal confrontation with Herod Antipas is briefly recounted in Josephus and the Gospels, was one of these prophetlike figures in the twenties of the first century C.E. Although John did not advise revolution, he did criticize society and thus, implicitly, the priests in Jerusalem and Herod Antipas. Anyone who calls for change is implicitly charging that something is wrong. John seems to have influenced an artisan named Jesus, from the Galilean village of Nazareth, who subsequently attracted a large following. Jesus was also one of these Jewish reformers, calling his people to repent of their sins and reaffirm their commitment to God's rule (the kingdom of God). At some point, he was understood by his followers to be the Messiah, the anointed leader sent by God to save Israel from infidelity and injustice. As such, he was like many other reformers, prophetic figures, and anointed leaders. In the decades after his death, Jesus' reform movement spread to Jews in surrounding countries, became a Jewish sect, incorporated Gentiles, organized itself into assemblies (churches), and finally, in the second century, became a religion for the most part separate from Judaism. A vigorous diaspora Jew named Paul was responsible for some of the spread of Jesus' teaching and the ferment in diaspora Jewish communities. In the 50s of the first century, an ascetic named Bannus lived in the (Judean?) desert, wearing clothes made of leaves or bark, eating food that grew wild, and frequently purifying himself in cold water. Josephus became his zealous follower for three years, before returning to Jerusalem and life among the governing class.[19] Bannus's program and purpose are unknown but must have involved some kind of faithful living of Jewish life in the face of social compromise within the Roman Empire.

Many other groups and trends enlivened Israel. Again and again, Josephus records the emergence of leaders who called Israel to rise up against the Roman Empire and met with defeat in the end. For example, when Herod was establishing himself as king in 37 B.C.E., he pursued Galilean brigands (landless peasants who took to the hills, lived off the land, and robbed the wealthy) in the wilderness, assaulted them in caves in the hillsides (J. W. 1 § 304–13), and finally captured their leader Ezekias (J. W. 1 § 204). When Herod died in 4 B.C.E., a number of uprisings took place. A tall, extraordinarily strong shepherd named Athronges claimed to be king and, with his four brothers, took over part of Judea until defeated by Roman troops (J. W. 2 § 60–65). A slave of Herod named Simon also proclaimed himself king, burned Herodian palaces at Jericho and elsewhere, and looted the countryside until he was finally defeated in battle (J. W. 2 § 57–59). Judas, the son of the brigand Ezekias, looted the armory in Sepphoris and terrorized Galilee (Ant. 17 § 271–72). When Herod's son Antipas was removed from his position as ruler of Judea and Samaria in 6 C.E. and replaced by a

Roman prefect, the Roman government took a census as a basis for taxation. In response, another Galilean named Judas led an uprising and, with the aid of a priest named Zadok, promoted a "philosophy" that was similar to the teaching of the Pharisees but proclaimed God alone as ruler (*Ant.* 18 § 4–10, 23–25). Although Josephus, the narrator of this story, strongly disapproved of this "fourth philosophy" and movement, it sounds like the Maccabees all over again. Other leaders proclaimed themselves king (Messiah) or a prophet from God and led the people into the wilderness in the hope that God would intervene. After the reign of Agrippa I (41–44 C.E.), the increasingly venal and unjust reigns of Roman procurators enraged the people and led to the rise of Sicarii, terrorists who assassinated their enemies.

At the beginning of the war against Rome in 66 C.E., various groups of peasants from Galilee, Idumea, and Judea gathered under local, popular leaders who both warred with one another and formed coalitions of Zealots who fought desperately against the Romans.[20] A man named Jesus was a brigand chief of a band of 800 men outside of Ptolemais (Acco) on the Mediterranean coast. John of Gischala in Galilee was Josephus's rival as leader in Galilee early in the revolt and subsequently escaped to Jerusalem where he used his contacts to overthrow the traditional leadership. He was the leader of one of the factions engaged in civil war within Jerusalem while the Romans were besieging it outside. Eleazar ben Simon was a sometime ally of John and then a rival leader of a splinter faction of the Zealots. Simon bar Giora, from Gerasa in Transjordan, gathered a brigand band and fought both the Romans and his fellow Jews in northern Judea, then in Idumea, and finally in Jerusalem. Numerous other leaders gathered followers during the disorder that accompanied the breakdown of the traditional Jerusalem leadership.

In summary, during the first century, the people of Israel had a number of strategies for preserving their identity and adapting their traditions in changing and often hostile circumstances. The temple priests and leading families, some of whom were Sadducees, negotiated with foreign governments, survived invasions and conquest, and responded to the attractions of Hellenistic culture with a dogged determination to survive and continue the sacrificial rituals and national laws of Israel. The Essenes, interpreting these policies and governance as a betrayal of God's will, established a pure priestly and lay community along the hot and barren shore of the Dead Sea, in order to await divine intervention against both the Romans and leaders in Jerusalem. The Pharisees sought to call Israel to greater fidelity to its covenant with God and stronger zeal in keeping the divine laws that guided Israel's life. The extension of priestly purity to the homes of ordinary Israelites sanctified people and land against the lure of Greek and Roman society and culture. Other popular leaders called the people to revolution, to expectation of the Messiah, to prophetic reform, or to passive resistance.

DEVIANCE AND SECTS

The variety, or to use a modern word, the pluralism in Judaism, in early Christianity, and in the Greco-Roman world as a whole forces us to think systematically about the relationships that hold society together or break it apart. For the individual or group in a time of peace and order, a society, culture, and religion simply *are*; it is "the way it is." One knows what a Jew is or what a Christian is. But, in times of disorder and change, the lines shift or become blurred. In times of conflict, the outsider becomes more prominent and demands to be explained. What do we make of others and of their otherness? What do we make of difference within our own community? How do we define ourselves? What is helpful and what is harmful?

We often call those who are "other" within a religion or community "sects," using the word pejoratively. We say they are deviant and imply that is bad. But sects can be looked at as groups responding to experiences and events in a way that differs from that of the majority. Deviants may be pernicious, but they may be creative and ahead of their time, too. The labeling of a group as a sect or as deviant usually involves a powerful majority trying to control a dissident minority. However, if conditions change, today's sect may be tomorrow's "orthodoxy." The shifting lines of sects and deviance in a society mark the tension points that will lead to growth and adaptation.[21] Paradoxically, a society's deviants are essential to its well-being. What a society considers deviant is intimately related to its identity, shows where it draws its boundaries, and exposes key structures and values in its social and symbolic system. What a society rejects partially defines what the society is.

In using deviance and sectarianism to understand the variety of Jewish groups in the first century, we must set deviance in a broad context. The struggle to define and sanction some behaviors and their attendant attitudes as deviant is always political (in the broad sense) and involves a power struggle for control of society.[22] Competing political interest groups promote particular modes of living; they symbolize society in coherent ways and condemn others who are different. Far from being subjective, foolish debates about preferences, these conflicts concern the basic shape of society, the relationships that will hold the society together, and the symbolic universe, which makes sense out of the flux of life. Much of our behavior and thinking is in itself ambiguous and indifferent. Thus, defining deviance is a struggle to bring order to human activities and the meanings we see in them. By defining deviant behavior, a society is aided in limiting the virtually infinite range of custom and outlook to a finite and coherent whole. It is a sign that a society has voluntarily restricted itself to a constant and stable pattern of activity.

Deviance is a necessary part of a functioning society in several senses.[23] Specifically, it is part of the larger social processes associated with stability and change, continuity and adaptation. It keeps

the society from rigidifying and failing to fulfill its necessary func-
tions. In the present case, Jews in Palestine and southern Syria had
to adapt, or perhaps better, to reconstitute their symbolic worlds,
and their social–political worlds as well, in the aftermath of the destruction of the temple and its leadership. Jerusalem, the symbolic
and political center of Palestinian Judaism, was eliminated with
grave community consequences that had to be met with innovative
solutions drawn from the tradition. Jewish literature of the period,
including the Mishnah (c. 200 C.E.) and the Gospel of Matthew
(c. 90 C.E.), testify to diverse approaches adopted by different Jewish
groups.[24]

In any social system, especially one in crisis like the Palestinian
Jewish social system after the destruction of the temple, what is
within the boundaries of the society and what is not, what is deviant and what is accepted is a matter of dispute. The competing rabbinic, apocalyptic, revolutionary, and Christian Jewish movements
are a rich field for analysis.

Deviant groups or sects come in a variety of shapes.[25] Some
seek to change the world. The revolutionist awaits the destruction
of the social order by divine forces. Apocalyptic groups fit this
type. The introversionist withdraws from the world into a purified
community. The Essenes fit this type. The reformist seeks gradual,
divinely revealed alterations in society. The Pharisees and Jesus
with his disciples probably fit this type. The subjectivist or conversionist sect seeks change in the person through emotional transformation now, with salvation presumed to follow in the future
after evil has been endured. Because of alienation from society, a
new community is formed. Early Christians fit this type. Some
sects seek to change the individual's relationship with the world
or society. The manipulationist seeks happiness by a transformed
subjective orientation that will control evil. Ancient Gnostics fit
this type, as do many new-age movements. The thaumaturgical
response seeks relief from specific ills by special, not general dis-

pensation. Magicians and healers, including some rabbis and Jesus, fit this type. These categories are not totally separate from one another, nor are they rigid. A group can have more than one response to the world at one time. At different times, groups having changing relationships with other parts of society and have to meet new challenges from outside society. The Roman Empire, wars, economic distress, population shifts, and so on, all caused cultural and religious shifts.

We turn now to the two most successful Jewish reform movements of the first century. The Pharisees led a long-lasting reform movement that sought to influence the government and people. The Pharisees actually gained power briefly twice, under John Hyrcanus (134–4 B.C.E.) and Alexandra (76–67 B.C.E.). They used the biblical laws and temple purity and holiness as guides to creating a holy, sanctified, faithful, renewed community of Jews, absorbing from Hellenism that which was digestible and rejecting that which was not. Kindness to their fellow Jews, responsibility for their lives, and the hope of life after death guided their actions. The first-generation Jesus movement in Palestine was most probably a reformist movement, within Judaism, characterized by thaumaturgical and millennial hopes. Jesus is pictured as preaching a more satisfying way of living Judaism, that is, a reformed Judaism. He addressed people's needs by miraculous cures and also by offering comfort and solace to those in distress. In addition, although not an active revolutionary leader, he promised and threatened an apocalyptic, revolutionary society with a new economic, political, and religious order ruled by God (the kingdom of God). This kingdom would sweep away the evils of this world. As the Jesus movement moved out of Palestine, it took on more aspects of a conversionist movement, leaving the millennial/revolutionist emphasis in the background (with the notable exception of the Book of Revelation). Typical of members of religious movements and sects, the early Christians did not achieve relief through palpable divine intervention, but the intellectual and emotional engagement with such hopes gave the community a sense of the future.

CREATIVITY, ADAPTATION, AND CHANGE

Even though deviant positions are often spoken of as outside the pale, sociologically and historically they are part of the whole. For example, Reform Judaism is rejected by some very orthodox Jews today as deviant and not authentically Jewish, yet even to those rejecting Reform Judaism, the members of that movement are Jews. The same may be said of the acceptance of the Reformation churches by the Roman Church, which previously condemned them as heretical sects. "Deviant groups" modify a social, political, or religious system when they judge that it does not make sense or does not work, but they build their new world with materials from the old world they share with those who have declared them deviant.

The deviance that is always part of society has predictable effects on society. Even though those in control often wish to eliminate deviance and see it as an evil, deviance is caused by social relationships and has both beneficent and negative effects on society. If there is a quantitatively and qualitatively small amount of marginal deviance that can be controlled by the majority, then deviance helps to define and strengthen social boundaries and promote cohesion. If there is a large amount of fundamental deviance, this is a sign of and a cause of significant social change.

Despite all the animus and conflict against government and empire in first-century Judaism, do not imagine that these reformist groups in Israel had returned to a pristine, non-Hellenistic form of Judaism. They adapted to their world and forged new social and intellectual arrangements that allowed their traditions and communities to survive. For example, the Essenes, who made their home away from Jerusalem by the Dead Sea, were significantly influenced by Greco-Roman society. The water works and industrial installations at Qumran and Ain Feshka reflect Hellenistic technology. The military equipment and tactics pictured in the *War Scroll* reflect Hellenistic or Roman models. Documents at Qumran are preserved in Hebrew, Aramaic, and Greek. The very formation of voluntary organizations with rules and membership requirements by the Pharisees, Essenes, and early Church is a Greek phenomenon used by traditional Jews against Hellenization. Usually one's way of life, religion, and culture were fixed by birth, but in the Hellenistic period more flexibility and mobility were fostered. People who were uprooted or conquered often chose new ways of life or cults, philosophies, and new religious movements.

For many, Christianity and Judaism were two of those religious movements that gained new adherents. The stress on individual conversion and commitment and on the pursuit of wisdom as a systematic, comprehensive understanding of God, humans, and the world owes much to the Greeks. Interest in fate and predestination, in astronomy, astrology, and related sciences, derives partly from the Persian and Greek influences of previous centuries. Many Jews became interested in new ways of living Judaism. Many Gentiles became interested in Judaism's monotheism, sexual restraint, Sabbath observance, commandments, and Bible through synagogues or through sister assemblies that taught the version of Judaism propounded by Jesus of Nazareth. The elements of Judaism handed on in the postexilic period were understood and lived in many forms with productive results.

For Discussion

1. What was the status of Jews in the Roman Empire during the first century?

2. How pluralistic was Judaism at the time of Jesus? Can you give some examples?

3. What was the geographical, social–political, and economic makeup of Galilee in the first century? How does this influence your understanding of Jesus and the area from which he came?

4. How did apocalyptic literature and imagery influence the reform movements within Judaism at the time of Jesus?

5. Name the various reformist movements of the first century. What were their basic teachings and understandings about life and religion? To which group was Jesus most likely akin?

6. Why are the terms "deviance" and "sectarianism" helpful in understanding the variety of Jewish groups in the first century? Could the followers of the Jesus movement be labeled by these terms?

7. From reading this chapter, what new understandings do you have about the Judaisms of the time of Jesus?

PART TWO

THE JEWISHNESS
OF JESUS

3

THE JEWISHNESS OF JESUS: COMMANDMENTS CONCERNING INTERPERSONAL RELATIONS

LAWRENCE H. SCHIFFMAN

◼

In a famous article by the late Rabbi Joseph Soloveitchik, Dean of the Rabbinical School of Yeshiva University, the main Orthodox Rabbinical Seminary in this country, there is a discussion of the ground rules for interfaith discussion.[1] In reading over this article recently, it struck me how much our original dialogue session and this entire program conformed to these goals. Rabbi Soloveitchik spoke of the need for each religious community to be allowed to speak on its own terms; the need for equality, that neither side should begin as an inferior; the need to define each faith thoroughly and in detail, and only then to be able to discuss matters of cooperation on which the faiths would come to agree. In that spirit, I think our opportunity to study together certain things that deal with Jesus and Judaism and Christianity is a very important step. I have always found that when we occupy ourselves in a joint learning experience, we can often create more goodwill than would result from whatever we might say.

My earliest encounters with the questions posed here were as a child seeking to understand how Jesus, whom we saw as the founder of another faith, could be understood in the context of Jewish religious tradition. After all, we knew him to have been a Jew. It was abundantly clear that virtually all of what he was said to have uttered and done really were part of this Jewish religious tradition. We generally thought, even without knowing much about New Testament scholarship, that Christianity had taken Jesus' teachings and made them into that "other religion," the holidays which we as Jews did not observe and the teachings which we did not accept.

I later came to realize that perhaps one has to temper this impression a bit, but the general notion—whether we speak of the commandments between humans and God or those "between human and human"[2]—that Jesus is, indeed, to be placed within the Jewish tradition, is basically correct. In a history of Second Temple and rabbinic Judaism that I wrote,[3] I included a section on the rise of Christianity, because Christianity in its early days is to be seen as a Jewish movement. It is clear, however, that despite my childhood perceptions, Christianity—and even, by the way, rabbinic Judaism—saw Jesus in a very different light as time went on. What was Jesus in his own time? We seek to answer only one small part of that question in investigating his relationship to the traditional Jewish commandments between human and human or, better, to the commandments pertaining to human relationships, the social message of ancient Judaism.

One cannot speak about laws governing interpersonal relationships without speaking a bit more about the social context in which Jesus grew up. Some have attempted to claim that virtually every social notion in the New Testament was an original creation and that nothing was owed to Judaism. On the contrary, both the social context of Jesus in his lifetime and his teachings reflect the Judaism of his time.

Although the task of creating a biography of Jesus is nearly impossible because of the mixture of fact and myth in virtually all our data, certain facts are known. He was part of the rural or village culture of northern Palestine, what we generally call Galilee, in the first century. He, or his father, was connected with carpentry or some related craft (depending on how we want to define the Greek terminology in the New Testament), and he apparently grew up imbibing many common Jewish traditions.[4] He may have given greater emphasis to some of these ideas, but the views attributed to Jesus in the New Testament are not surprising; these are traditional Jewish notions that were widespread in large segments of the Jewish community. Some examples will demonstrate that, in regard to social matters, he can be placed in the camp closest to the Pharisees and furthest from such sectarians as those who left us the Dead Sea Scrolls.

It should come as no surprise that Jesus' teachings have much in common with the Pharisees. The polemics in the earlier texts are against the Pharisees, the group with whom he had contact.[5] Polemics serve to differentiate oneself from others with whom one might be confused. They serve to define and separate one's own group as opposed to groups that might be mistaken for it or against which it might be revolting. The groups in question have to be fairly close in outlook and structure for this relationship to obtain. For example, we do not generally expect to find the Democratic party arguing against communism in modern-day America. Rather, they argue against the Republican party. Whoever wrote these accounts of Jesus portrays him as constantly arguing with the Pharisees although they are closest to him on social issues.

A few examples may easily be drawn from the Sermon on the Mount. Jesus makes some seemingly extreme comments about anger, saying that anger can be seen as almost like murder (Matt

5:21-22). Such statements fall fairly close to some statements of the later Talmudic sages, such as "Whoever gets angry, all kinds of (punishments of) Gehenna (hell) rule over him. . . . Whoever gets angry, even the Divine Presence must not be important to him";[6] or "Whoever gets angry, it is as if he worshiped idols."[7] In the same passage, Jesus speaks strongly against one who insults his fellow, to which we can compare, "One who embarrasses his fellow in public . . . even though he has learned much Torah and done many good deeds, has no portion in the world to come;"[8] and "One who embarrasses his fellow in public goes down to Gehenna and will not come up; it is as if he has murdered (him)."[9]

We should not expect exact correspondence between what Jesus says and what the rabbis say. First, the rabbis are chronologically later, even if we find that many rabbinic traditions reflect the general Pharisaic milieu of earlier on. Hence, similar ideas may have been available in different formulations in Jesus' own time. Second, although Jesus was well aware of many Jewish traditions of his time, as any committed Jew might have been, he was surely not a rabbinically trained disciple who would have drawn his teachings from a proto-Mishnah or Talmud. But Pharisaic values were to a great extent the milieu of Palestinian Judaism of this period and, therefore, we can expect him to reflect many of these teachings.

In another example of teachings regarding the relationship between persons, Jesus speaks very strongly against the swearing of oaths (Matt 5:33-37). Oaths in Judaism are not to be taken lightly. According to Jewish law, a person can forbid something to someone else or to himself. In first-century Jewish society, oaths and vows were widely used for mundane purposes.[10] For example, if someone invited a friend to his house for dinner and that person did not want to come and kept giving excuses for not accepting, the inviter would say to him, "I enjoin you that if you do not come to my house for dinner, you can never have anything that belongs to me or benefit from anything that belongs to me forever." If this pair happened to have extensive relationships or did business together, the invited party would have second thoughts and quickly accept the invitation and come to dinner.[11]

Such oaths were a part of the culture. Jesus was not alone in speaking against them. In the Talmud, there are statements to the effect that anybody who swears oaths of this kind, even if he keeps them, is a sinner.[12] Indeed, Jesus' statement deals with this type of oath. It is most significant that we find the Pharisees taking a stand against such oaths as well,[13] partly because of their concern for the problem of taking, in God's name, oaths that may not be fulfilled, and partly because such oaths can be used to separate people one from another.

We all know that Jesus speaks at length of loving one's enemies (Matt 5:43-48; Luke 6:27-28, 32-36). Much of this is derived from statements in the Hebrew Bible requiring giving aid to one's enemy under certain circumstances (Exod 23:4-5; Prov 25:21-22) and not rejoicing when one's enemy is in trouble (Prov 24:17-18). But the rabbis speak of these matters in numerous Talmudic passages.[14] They teach us that we have to love the enemy even while hating what he does. We may hate the activity, sin, but never the sinner. The entire notion of even hating an enemy is decried over and over in rabbinic sources. This is all based on the prohibition of hatred in Leviticus (19:17). Constantly, we encounter rabbinic exegesis of biblical stories in which conflict is always being reduced and in which the biblical figures are portrayed as making up with their enemies.

Halakah, Jewish law, requires that we apologize to our enemies against whom we have sinned and specifies that if they come to us, we must forgive them.[15] Let me illustrate this with a true story. A good friend of mine called me up once and said that he did not know what to do. There was a man who was asking his forgiveness and he could not bring himself to forgive him. The man began asking his forgiveness the week before Rosh Hashanah, the Jewish New Year, and up to the day before Yom Kippur, the Day of Atonement, my friend had not been able to forgive him. He had apparently suffered a financial loss because of this man's transgression. He wanted to know from me what his obligations were under Jewish law. I told him that he had no choice but to find a way to be able to forgive him, not because he did not believe that what the offender did was wrong, but because it was his obligation according to Jewish law to forgive the man who had sinned against him. That is no different from what Jesus teaches. One could say that I learned it from the New Testament, but it is all over rabbinic literature and it is a requirement of Jewish law. My friend called me after Yom Kippur and he told me, "I want you to know that Yom Kippur night the man came and asked me if I would forgive him and I said no. Again, in the morning, the man came and I said no. By the afternoon, I went over to him and said, 'Yes, I have finally come to be able to forgive you. I am still resentful of what you did but I understand that you deserve a new beginning.'" This is no different from what is being taught in the New Testament. It is classical Judaism still being practiced today.

Another excellent example is almsgiving, particularly as regards giving in private. Maimonides, the great medieval Jewish philosopher and codifier of Jewish law, sets down the law that it is obligatory to give charity in private. He goes even further and says that the greatest form of charity, with the exception of entering into a partnership with the poor person, is when the recipient does not know who gave the gift to him or her.[16] This is the very same notion that Jesus teaches (Matt 6:1-4). All of the stress on almsgiving and how to give charity is Pharisaic Judaism.[17] It is true that our sources for Pharisaic charity practices date only from the period of the Mishnah, somewhat later than the time of Jesus, but there is no question that these practices were in full practice during Jesus' life. Another example is the Golden Rule, which the New Testament states as follows: "Whatever you wish that people would do to you, do so to them" (Matt 7:12; Luke 6:31), concluding in Matthew with the words, "for this is the law and the prophets." This pithy statement is by no means original to Jesus.[18] It is found as well in the famous statement of Hillel, which says exactly the same thing: "What is hateful to you, do not do to your neighbor."[19] Further, the entire idea derives from the book of Leviticus: "Love your neighbor as yourself" (Lev 19:18). Throughout the Hebrew Bible and the Pharisaic–rabbinic corpus, this point is emphasized. The sage Rabbi Akiva, after quoting Leviticus 19:18, added: "This is a fundamental summary of the Torah."[20] There is absolutely no question that Jesus shares these ethical ideas with his Jewish background and, I would emphasize, with the Pharisaic background.[21]

Some would emphasize the difference between the positive formulation in the New Testament, "Love thy neighbor as thyself," and the negative formulation in the Jewish version, "What is hateful to your neighbor, do not do unto him." As far as I am concerned, this is nothing but polemic. Let me explain why. Let us remember that a Jew living in the first century of our era in Palestine would have been in the synagogue and would have heard the Torah read regularly. The New Testament, which, by the way, is one of our best sources for Jewish practices in this period, tells us that Jesus was present during Torah readings (Luke 4:16; cf. Matt 13:54, Mark 6:2, and Acts 15:21). This is testimony to the centrality of public reading of the law in the synagogue service at this early date. An average synagogue-attending Jew, hearing the entire Torah most probably every three years as was the practice in Palestine in rabbinic times, would have been thoroughly familiar with the Torah text. Such a person would have known that he was commanded to love his neighbor, that is, his fellow Jew, and that a second passage commanded him to love the non-Jews among whom he lived (Lev 19:34).

The other formulation, the negative phrasing, "What is hateful to your neighbor, do not do unto him," is an Aramaic statement occurring in the context of what is probably a third- or fourth-century retelling in Aramaic of some stories about the sage Hillel, who lived in the time somewhat before Jesus. Yet earlier parallels are known from classical Greek literature and, most importantly, from earlier Jewish literature. This formulation already exists in Tobit 4:15, an Aramaic book composed probably in the first half of the second century B.C.E., where it says, "What you hate, do not do to anyone."[22] The Jewish philosopher Philo (c. 20 B.C.E.–50 C.E.) made exactly the same statement[23] with an addition paralleling Matthew: "Moreover, it is ordained in the laws themselves that no one shall do to his neighbor what he would be unwilling to have done to himself." But the operative statement for Jesus' Jewish contemporaries would have been that of the Hebrew Bible itself, "Love your neighbor as yourself." A positive formulation of this notion is also given by the Mishnaic rabbis in the Ethics of the Fathers, "May the honor of your neighbor be as important to you as your own."[24]

Why did the negative formulation come into being? It seems to me that it was precisely because someone wanted to get across the other side of the statement, namely that whatever it is that you would not want your neighbor to do to you, you should not do to him. This is simply biblical interpretation that presumes the original biblical statement.[25] This explanation is confirmed by Philo's statement, after the negative formulation, that "it is ordained in the laws themselves."

My colleague Professor Sanders called attention in his remarks to the statement attributed to Jesus that, "It is not what goes into the mouth that defiles a man, but what goes out of the mouth" (Matt 15:11, 17-19; Mark 7:15, 18-23). Sanders suggests that no Pharisaic Jew would be able to agree with such a statement.[26] It may or may not be of much significance, but one proof of how Jewish this statement may be is the fact that I quote it often. Let me explain. In a Jewish context, where the audience properly understands the significance of the dietary laws and shares in their observance, the point of this statement is to emphasize that the true purpose of these laws is the creation of a refined and ethical human being.

This is exactly the way I understand the gospel passage. Simply to eat kosher food, if one does not understand what this set of ritual requirements is designed to teach, is a meaningless act.

Now let me draw your attention to a Midrashic parallel.[27] The Midrash is interpreting the words of 2 Samuel 22:31, Psalm 18:30, "The word of the Lord is refined." It takes this statement as relating to the laws of ritual slaughter. According to Jewish law, when one slaughters a four-legged animal, usually cattle, one must cut both the windpipe and the esophagus in order to render the animal instantly unconscious and avoid pain to the animal. If one slaughters a fowl, which has a less complex nervous system, then one need sever only one or the other. This law leads the rabbis to make the following observation: What is the difference to God if one severs one or both? The answer given is that "the commandments were given only to refine humanity."

In my view, this is the very same point made in the statement attributed to Jesus. These laws are designed to bring about the moral refinement of the person who observes them. Indeed, Maimonides makes this point emphatically at the end of the section of his code of Jewish law pertaining to kosher food: "Everyone who is scrupulous regarding these matters brings holiness and greater purity to himself and purifies his soul for the sake of the Holy One; blessed be He, as it says (in the Torah), 'You shall purify yourselves and be holy for I (God) am holy'" (Lev 11:44).[28] What he means here is this: Do not believe that it is enough just to eat these pure foods. These restrictions are supposed to mold a type of personality, a life of ethics, and a way of thinking about God and His creatures. I see the extreme, perhaps shocking, statement of Jesus as saying the very same thing and lying squarely within the Jewish tradition.

Lest I mislead you, I certainly recognize that when one reads the statements attributed to Jesus on matters pertaining to relations between people, one finds a few glaring examples of difference. One of them, which we do not have time to unravel now, is

Jesus' apparent rejection of his family in favor of his disciples (Matt 12:46-50; Mark 3:31-35; Luke 8:19-21). These texts show the unmistakable influence of several passages from the Hebrew Bible, specifically the account of the Golden Calf (Exod 32:27-28) and its reflection in the Blessing of Moses (Deut 33:8-9). This attitude on the part of Jesus or the Gospel writers cannot be squared with the contemporary Pharisaic–rabbinic approach. I am not certain how to explain this passage or, to put it otherwise, whether it can be explained away. I simply present this as an example to point out that we cannot simplistically assume that every word relating to commandments between one person and another in the Gospels and attributed to Jesus is in agreement with the Pharisaic–rabbinic tradition.

But the overwhelming majority of this material pertaining to the social message of the New Testament does place Jesus in that Pharisaic-rabbinic context. What is the alternative that I am essentially arguing against? It goes like this: Jesus wandered around in the area of the Dead Sea, maybe before or after his baptism by John the Baptist, and there came into contact with the Dead Sea sectarians, usually identified with the Essenes. There he read the scrolls and imbibed the teachings of these "proto-Christians," left Qumran, and went out to teach Christianity. According to such a view, Christianity would be a copy of, or expansion on, the religion of the sect of the Dead Sea Scrolls.

What is the problem with such a view? How about the passages in the Qumran sectarian texts that say that members of the group should hate everybody who is not a member? How about the notion in the *War Scroll* from Qumran that, in the end of days, all those who are not members of the group, first non-Jews and then Jews, will die? How about the notion that one is prohibited from having social or even economic contact with anybody who is not a member of the sect? These notions of the sect are in stark contrast to the preaching of Jesus according to the Gospels.

To speak briefly about ritual, the Qumran sect had purity laws that were much stricter and infinitely more separatist than those of the Pharisees. Yet we all know the New Testament accounts of how Jesus would constantly eat with people whom the Pharisees would have stayed away from for reasons of purity law; instead, Jesus reached out to them to bring them his message.[29] In contrast, the Dead Sea sect seems to have taken views diametrically opposed to those attributed to Jesus on this matter. Attempts to place him in the context of this sect, therefore, do not seem to be too plausible. Christianity has traditionally defined itself, like the Pharisaic-rabbinic tradition, with an ethic of much greater openness and, indeed, love. This ethic is shared with and derived from the Pharisaic tradition. To a great extent, I think one could argue that much of this ethic is simply valid interpretation of the Hebrew Scriptures.

In any case, the milieu in terms of ethics and, in our case, of the social vision of Jesus is the Pharisaic–rabbinic one. I also will say that when one lines up disputes regarding matters of Jewish law in which we have a position of Jesus, a position of the Pharisees, and a position of the Dead Sea sect, Jesus comes out on what we may call the left, the lenient side; the Pharisees occupy the middle ground; and the Dead Sea sect is on the right, adopting the strictest ruling.

Let me give an example from the domain of Sabbath law. May you take an animal out of a pit on the Sabbath if the animal is going to die? A statement attributed to Jesus says that there is no question that one may take an animal out of the pit (Matt 12:11; Luke 14:5). The Pharisees require that some pillows or boards be put down, in an attempt to get the animal to climb out on its own.[30] The Dead Sea sect takes the view that one may not do anything that might impinge on the sanctity of the Sabbath even if the animal would die.[31]

I will include one more example because it gives me a chance to offer a somewhat different interpretation from the one just stated, namely, Jesus' picking of grain on the Sabbath (Matt 12:1-8;

Mark 2:23-28; Luke 6:1-5). There is a long explanation in the New Testament text about why, in particular circumstances, it was permissible. Part of the answer Matthew gives in the name of Jesus is that the priests in the temple slaughter animals on the Sabbath and otherwise violate the Sabbath regulations. The text is asserting that, according to Jewish law, positive commandments outweigh negative commandments. Therefore, picking grain on the Sabbath to provide for hungry people was ruled acceptable by the Gospel of Matthew. This indeed follows from the argument put forward in all three accounts (Matt 12:3-4; Mark 2:25-6; Luke 6:3-4) to the effect that David took of the bread of the presence to feed the hungry men who were with him (1 Sam 21:1-6). Again, the import is that this action, normally considered a sacrilege, was permissible in order to feed the hungry. To the early Christians, therefore, picking of grain on the Sabbath was permitted on the assumption that the positive commandment of feeding the hungry outweighs the negative commandment of not harvesting on the Sabbath. Such a view is much more lenient than that of the Pharisees who would say that, except in the case of real danger, it is forbidden to violate the Sabbath restrictions to feed a hungry person.

In the same way, the rabbis ruled that it is forbidden to heal on the Sabbath unless there is danger. Danger for the rabbis constitutes even danger to a limb or an organ of the body. If a person has an earache, for example, he is required to ride to the doctor on the Sabbath, even though that would normally constitute a Sabbath violation. The Dead Sea sect would say that one should make every attempt to save the person while avoiding every possible violation of the Sabbath. This view is much more severe than that of the rabbis, who advise ignoring the Sabbath restrictions and moving immediately to save the life or limb. Jesus, as I said, is to the left of this. So, not only in the ethical sphere (which I addressed at length earlier) does Jesus come out much closer to the Pharisees, but I would argue that on the continuum of the ritual sphere, Jesus would, likewise, come out much closer to the Pharisees than he would to the Dead Sea sect. Therefore, I personally reject the attempt to claim a close connection between Jesus and the Qumran sect.

Although it is not our topic at present, I do feel the need to remark on the significance of the Dead Sea Scrolls for understanding early Christianity. I must emphasize that, in terms of the dating of the scrolls, the documents were composed before the rise of Christianity. If Jesus was not a member of the Qumran sect, as we have said, do the Dead Sea Scrolls teach us anything about Jesus and early Christianity? I am not going to discuss examples, but I want to be certain that no one gets the wrong impression. The scrolls certainly do provide us with background for the career and teachings of Jesus and for understanding the New Testament.

Because the Dead Sea Scrolls contain much material from a variety of groups, they illumine the entire religious landscape of the Judaism that served as the background for Christianity. Much of this material is even earlier than the founding of the sect in the aftermath of the Maccabean Revolt (168–164 B.C.E.). Books like Enoch and Jubilees, and other apocryphal and apocalyptic works, contribute to the religious milieu that informs early Christianity, affecting both the authors and the later tradents (deliverers) of what became the New Testament. But the notion that somehow Jesus came out of that sect seems to be belied by the legal material regarding commandments both between people and those between people and God which we have been studying.

Having said all this, I want to repeat my conclusion briefly: Investigation of the views attributed to Jesus on the commandments pertaining to interpersonal relationships places Jesus squarely in the Jewish ethical world of his times and, particularly, that which derives from the Pharisaic–rabbinic tradition.

If such a degree of commonality existed, then it is important to clarify why the Jewish people did not "accept Jesus." This is a question that has to be faced frankly yet respectfully. Jews and Judaism believed that the Hebrew prophets foretold a certain sequence of events that would signal and evidence the onset of the messianic era. In fact, belief in the coming redemption was virtually uniform among the various circles of Jews in Hasmonean and Roman times. During his lifetime, Jesus himself is said to have advanced a variety of teachings which, as we have said, were very much within the scope of Pharisaic–rabbinic tradition. However, either through certain teachings attributed to him, which indicated that he seemed to view the "kingdom" as already oncoming, or through things said by his disciples at a later stage, it became clear that the Christian view of messianism was not the one that the Jews had expected. Hence, when the messiahship of Jesus became a major tenet of Christianity, Judaism and the Jewish community did not feel that Jesus had lived up to the requirements for a messianic figure as understood by them from the prophets and, therefore, they did not take him to be the Messiah. When, somewhat later, some of his followers attributed to him aspects of divinity, this concept violated the Jewish understanding of what monotheism was and therefore was unacceptable to Jews. For this variety of reasons, Jews did not and do not accept the messiahship or the divinity of Jesus.

Enough was unique about Jesus so that he was not accepted by his Jewish compatriots. However one wants to interpret the various events described in the New Testament, one thing is clear: The majority of Palestinian Jews did not follow this teacher. After his death, the majority of Jews continued not to follow him, and Judaism concluded that Christianity was "the other."[32] The ancient Jews must have perceived and experienced a great deal about Jesus and Christianity that they saw as different from what was going on in the Jewish environment. We do not have time here to discuss the question of to what extent the messianic pretensions placed in Jesus' mouth in the New Testament (for example, Matt 11:2-6; Luke 7:18-23) reflect his own teachings or later views of what happened to him; this is a matter in which I would not claim any expertise. But, soon after his death, the perception of him in that messianic framework must have influenced the fact that Jews saw him as "the other." There is, therefore, no question that even though his social message may have essentially been that of Pharisaism, he differed from that tradition in other ways and regarding other kinds of issues.

One basic problem still remains, and I want to put it on the table because I think it will make some of our later discussions easier. If I have drawn an accurate portrait, then one would assume that there would never have been any conflict between Judaism and Christianity. Indeed, we would expect all Christians to be devout Jews. But clearly this is not the case. We do not have time to discuss the extent to which, and the manner in which, later tradition and events that took place either at the close of Jesus' life or shortly thereafter led to the schism that we know of and then to the problems of anti-Semitism with which we are all too familiar. These have today become more and more prominent in our minds as our country opens the Holocaust Museum and at the same time debates what to do about "ethnic cleansing" in Bosnia. We are in a strange position. On the one hand, we need to stress, both for academic reasons, because it seems to be the objective truth, and for interreligious reasons as well, the Jewishness of Jesus and the fact that his views were, to a great extent, based on the Judaism of his age. On the other hand, we observe that Christianity moved in a very different direction as it continued to develop. In my view, by the year 135 C.E., the close of the Bar Kokhba revolt, there had taken place an irreconcilable religious schism in terms of our varying ideologies and beliefs.

The purpose of our accenting the common elements, therefore, is not to deny or obscure the differences which can never be reversed, but to try to reverse the negative ramifications that these differences have had in times and places much less tolerant than our own. We seek to undo the ramifications of struggle, dispute, hatred, and Holocaust and to reverse them in favor of a notion that recognition of our common origins and of those things which the founding figure of Christianity shared with the Judaism from which he emerged will bring us to greater hope for a future of commonality. In this effort, we may be guided by the agenda that Judaism set and Christianity received: on the one hand, love of God, and on the other, love of fellow human beings.

For Discussion

1. Why is Christianity in its early days to be seen as a Jewish movement? Does such an understanding change your approach to Jews and Christians?

2. How did both the social context of Jesus in his lifetime as well as his teachings reflect the Judaism of his time?

3. In what ways was Jesus closely related to the Pharisees and their practice of faith?

4. What is the relationship of Jesus' teachings, found in the New Testament, to the teachings found in the Talmud? How does this relationship change your understanding of Jesus?

5. Do Jesus' teachings on forgiveness, almsgiving, and the Golden Rule have Jewish roots? If so, what is the implication for Christians and their approach to both Jews and Judaism?

6. Why is it invalid simplistically to assume that every word relating to commandments in the Gospels which is attributed to Jesus is in agreement with the Pharisaic–rabbinic tradition?

7. What is the problem with the view that Christianity is a copy of, or an expansion on, the religion of the sect of the Dead Sea Scrolls?

8. What is the significance of the Dead Sea Scrolls for understanding the rise of Christianity?

9. Why did the Jewish people not "accept Jesus" as Messiah and as being divine?

10. From reading this chapter, what new understandings and insights do you have about Jesus, his teachings, and their Jewish roots?

4

JESUS AND THE FIRST TABLE
OF THE JEWISH LAW

E. P. SANDERS

■

The two pillars of Judaism are the election and the law: God called Abraham and his descendants to be his people; a few centuries later he gave them the law by the hand of Moses. If we are to discuss Jesus' Jewishness, we must address these two topics. Because these are short essays, however, each can deal with only some of the most crucial points. Professor Schiffman and I have agreed to discuss Jesus' stance toward different parts of the Jewish law. I shall explain the basic division of the law and shall discuss the first half.

THE TWO TABLES

The Jewish law falls naturally into two parts, often called "tables." The first table consists of the commandments that govern relations between humans and God, and the second table contains commandments governing relations among humans. The division can be seen, for example, in the Ten Commandments (Exod 20:2-17;

Deut 5:7-21): "You shall have no other gods before me" begins the
first table; "You shall not kill" begins the second. It is probable that,
in Jesus' day, all learned Jews knew this division into tables and
the contents of each. How many Jews were learned? I think that
most of them were educated enough to know about the division
of the law and most of the principal laws in each table. Some, of
course, were especially learned and were able to teach the law; the
rest were fairly learned because they listened as it was taught in the
synagogues. Philo of Alexandria, a very wealthy man who was as
learned as he was rich, maintained that, on the Sabbath, Jews
throughout the world gathered in "schools" where they learned
what he calls their "ancestral philosophy." This "philosophy," he
notes, falls under two headings: duty toward God and duty toward
other humans;[1] that is, the Jewish "philosophy" consisted of the two
tables of the Jewish law.

When they wanted to summarize these two divisions of the law,
Jews quoted two central passages from their Scripture (the Christian "Old Testament"). One is found in Deuteronomy 6, the famous
passage called the *Shema* in Hebrew, from its first word, "Hear."
These are the first two verses of the passage:

> Hear, O Israel: The Lord is our God, the Lord alone. You shall love
> the Lord your God with all your heart, and with all your soul, and
> with all your might. (Deut 6:4-5)[2]

The second passage enjoins, as Philo put it, fellowship with all humans and *philanthrōpia*, love of humanity.[3] It is "Love your neighbor
as yourself" (Lev 19:18). Strictly speaking, Leviticus 19:18 requires
Jews to love only their "neighbors," that is, fellow Jews. But a few
verses later comes the requirement to "love the alien as yourself"
(Lev 19:34). Philo, along with other thoughtful Jews, read these and
other verses as divine commandments requiring love of all humanity. We see this especially clearly when we note that Philo and others sometimes used an epigram based on both Leviticus 19:18 and

19:34, rather than quoting the passages. Three different sources offer us this epigrammatic summary (with only minor variations): "Do not do to anyone what you would hate that person to do to you."[4] "To anyone" shows that, whatever the original meaning of "neighbor" and "alien" in Leviticus 19, later Jews understood that God commanded them to show love to all humanity.

It is striking that two of the people to whom the epigram "Do not do" is attributed (Philo and Hillel) said that it summarized "the whole law." Logically, the epigram summarizes only the second table. If he were pressed on this point, probably Philo would have explained that loving treatment of others proves that one is devoted to God. In the decades after Jesus' time, some rabbis said that refusing to worship other gods was tantamount to obeying the whole law.[5] Logically (again), avoidance of idolatry shows only that one observes the commandments on the first table. But (these rabbis probably thought) people who worshiped only the true God would also keep his other commandments, including the commandments governing how to treat humans. Jews who used one saying as a summary of the whole law were not excluding other parts of the law; they regarded all the commandments as being implied by one of the great commandments.

JESUS AND THE TWO TABLES

Two passages in the Gospels indicate that Jesus agreed fully with the view of the law that I have exemplified by citing Philo and others. A scribe asked him, "Which commandment is the first of all?" Jesus answered:

> The first is, "Hear O Israel: The Lord our God, the Lord is one; and you shall love the Lord your God with all your heart, and with all your soul, and with all your mind, and with all your strength." The second is this, "You shall love your neighbor as yourself." There is no other commandment greater than these. (Mark 12:28-31)

The scribe agreed fully (as we should expect), and Jesus said that he was not far from the kingdom of God (Mark 12:32-34).[6] We see that Jesus was among those who knew that the law was divided into two tables and who knew the main biblical passages that summarize each. Implicit, of course, is his agreement that people should obey the laws on both of the two tables.

As did Philo, Jesus also offered a one-sentence epigram to summarize the whole law: "So whatever you wish that people would do to you, do so to them; for this is the law and the prophets" (Matt 7:12). Logically, this statement summarizes only the second table. Yet Jesus called it "the law and the prophets." This does not imply that he wished to cancel the laws on the first table, such as the requirement to serve the Lord alone. Rather, for homiletical purposes, he, like others, could use a summary of the second table to stand for the whole law; by implication, the commandment concerning treatment of other people includes the requirement to love the God who commanded love of one's neighbor.

In all of these cases—the passages from Leviticus, Deuteronomy, Philo, the Talmud, Tobit, and the Gospels—"love" does not mean only, or even primarily, an emotion. In Leviticus 19, the general commandment to love one's neighbor includes several very specific actions that demonstrate love: leave some of the harvest for the poor and the sojourner; do not lie, cheat, or steal; do not oppress your neighbor; pay a servant's wages promptly; care for the deaf and the blind; be impartial in judgment; do not slander (Lev 19:9-16). You should, to be sure, love your neighbor "in your heart" (Lev 19:17), but love is expressed by just and honest treatment. The love commandment is a summary; in the second half of the Ten Commandments and elsewhere we find specific behavioral requirements: honor your father and mother; do not kill; do not commit adultery; and the like (Exod 20:12-17; Deut 5:16-21).

Similarly, in the first half of the Ten Commandments there are specifics: have no other gods; do not make graven images; do not bow down to and worship idols; do not take God's name in vain; keep the Sabbath in honor of God (Exod 20:2-11; Deut 5:6-15). Observing these specific commandments demonstrates "love."

SPECIFIC ASPECTS OF THE FIRST TABLE

Today, when we read the second commandment, "You shall not bow down to [idols] or serve them" (Deut 5:9), we often do not consider the precise meaning of the word "serve" in Judaism and other ancient religions. It meant "serve by sacrificing to"; that is, "serve" refers to the cultic or ritual aspect of religion, the part having to do with priests, purification, and sacrificial slaughter. In the past few centuries, few terms have drawn as much censure in religious propaganda and polemic as "cult" and "ritual." Protestants have criticized Catholics for ritualism and externalism, and Protestants and Catholics have joined forces to criticize ancient Jews on the very same grounds. Propagandists usually assume that the targets of their attacks *substitute* external forms and rites for internal devotion, and then they regard the fact of ritual observances as proving a lack of correct inner piety. To many Protestants, the fact that Catholicism has a rite of penitence proves that Catholics do not truly repent in their hearts.

I do not doubt that, because human nature is what it is, there have always been some people who left their religion at the altar. It is not, however, the case that the rites of Catholicism destroy interior devotion, nor is it true that most Roman Catholics substitute cultic ritual for inner piety. It is just as indefensible to accuse ancient Judaism on this ground. Ancient Jews, in fact, recognized the danger and spent considerable time warning each other about it. Hosea depicted God as desiring love rather than sacrifice and knowledge of God rather than burnt offerings (Hos 6:6). Similarly, a few centuries later, Jesus ben Sira warned people not to say "He will consider the multitude of my gifts, and when I make an offering to the Most High

God he will accept it." God expects his worshipers to pray and to give alms to the poor (Ben Sira 7:9f.). Several decades later, the pseudonymous author of the *Epistle of Aristeas* wrote that Jews "honor God not with gifts or sacrifices, but with purity of heart and of devout disposition."[7] These passages do not mean that Hosea, Ben Sira, and Pseudo-Aristeas were against sacrifice; they were, rather, against sacrifice without love, devotion, purity of heart, and charitable acts. In ancient Hebrew parlance (as we shall see more fully below), "desire mercy *and not* sacrifice" meant "desire mercy *more than* sacrifice." Pseudo-Aristeas and Ben Sira both favored sacrifice, provided that it was offered in the right spirit (for example, *Ep. Aristeas* 170–71; Ben Sira 34:18-19; 35:12). These admonitions to put mercy, love, honesty, and interior devotion first did not stop with Ben Sira and Pseudo-Aristeas. In the centuries after Jesus, the rabbis endlessly urged the importance of "intention" and "directing the heart" when observing "external" practices.[8]

Now we shall turn our attention to the question of Jesus' attitude toward the first table of the Jewish law. Did he oppose any of its aspects? We start with sacrifice.

Jesus and Sacrifice

According to Matthew, Jesus quoted Hosea 6:6, "I desire mercy and not sacrifice," in two cases when his critics seemed to be lacking in mercy (Matt 9:13; 12:7). In neither case is sacrifice actually an issue, and these passages offer no direct information about Jesus' view of sacrifice. According to Mark 12:33, however, when Jesus used this prophetic passage he said that love "is *much more than* all whole burnt offerings and sacrifices." Mark's version corresponds to the original meaning of Hosea; there is no objection to sacrifice.

Other passages reveal that Jesus shared the view of Philo, Pseudo-Aristeas, the rabbis, and other Jews. The teaching that mentions sacrifice most directly is this:

60

If you are offering your gift at the altar, and there remember that your brother has something against you, leave your gift there before the altar and go; first be reconciled to your brother, and then come and offer your gift. (Matt 5:23-24.)

The "gift" here is probably a guilt offering, brought in order to complete the process of atonement for harming another person. The sacrifice did not count if the offender had not first compensated the person whom he had harmed and paid an additional twenty percent as a fine. This is clear in the biblical legislation itself (Lev 6:1-7), and we have already exemplified the general principle by citing Ben Sira and others. Philo put it this way:

The lawgiver [Moses] orders that forgiveness be extended to [a wrongdoer] on condition that he verifies his repentance not by a mere promise but by his actions, by restoring the deposit or the property which he has seized . . . or in any way usurped from his neighbour, and further has paid an additional fifth as a solatium for the offense. And when he has thus propitiated the injured person he must follow it up, says the lawgiver, by proceeding to the temple to ask for remission of his sins . . . (Philo, *Special Laws* 1.236f.)

Philo continues by noting that the transgressor must not only repent but also sacrifice a ram (*ibid.*)

Thus, although sacrifice is not a major topic of the teaching attributed to Jesus, Matthew 5:23-24 indicates that his views on it were precisely the same as those held by other Jewish thinkers and teachers.

Sacrifice is alluded to indirectly, but nevertheless positively, in another passage. Jesus healed a leper and then commanded him, "show yourself to the priest, and offer for your cleansing what Moses commanded, for a proof to the people" (Mark 1:40-44). "What Moses commanded" turns out to be sacrificial birds and lambs (Lev 14:1-32). Here again a saying attributed to Jesus presupposes acceptance of the Jewish sacrificial system.

Jesus and the Sabbath

The fourth of the Ten Commandments is the requirement to do no work on the seventh day of the week (Exod 20:8-11). The Sabbath loomed quite large in Jewish life in the first century. Despite its prominence in the Ten Commandments and the creation story (Gen 2:2-3), the Sabbath plays a very small role in most of the Hebrew Bible. We do not read, for example, that David or Hezekiah had to change his plans because of the Sabbath, nor is the Sabbath a major topic of the preexilic prophets. It appears that it became an important and distinctive feature of Jewish life during and after the Babylonian captivity.[9] From the time of the Hasmoneans (Maccabees) on, Jews agreed that it was illegal to wage war on the Sabbath unless they were directly attacked.[10] The major pious groups, the Pharisees and the Essenes, elaborated Sabbath law in various ways,[11] which shows that defining what was and was not permitted on the Sabbath was a topic of major concern during Jesus' lifetime. Everyone, even the most radical Essene or Pharisee, agreed that saving life overrides the Sabbath. This sounds precise, but in fact it is not. Can one work on the Sabbath in order to prevent life-threatening situations from arising? Pompey, the Roman general, knew of the Jewish Sabbath law, and when he besieged Jerusalem he built earthworks and brought up his engines of war on the Sabbath, when the Jews would not fire on his men.[12] We may well imagine that some Jews were arguing that moving catapults into range and bringing up a battering ram were *tantamount* to a direct assault, and that therefore they should attack the Romans on the Sabbath. This argument, if it was made, did not prevail; the Jews allowed the Romans to bring their heavy weapons up to the wall, and eventually Jerusalem fell to Pompey.

The question of invasion is only a dramatic instance of a general problem. Once appeals to *mitigating circumstances* are allowed, it is hard to know where to stop. I shall stay with Pompey's invasion in order to give hypothetical examples. The principle, to repeat, is that work is permitted in order to save life. Perhaps, then, the Jews should have attacked Pompey's men on the Sabbath while they were building the earthworks that would allow them to bring catapults and battering rams up to the wall. Perhaps the Jewish defenders should have attacked on a previous Sabbath, before the Romans reached Jerusalem. That is, possibly the Sabbath should be violated in order to keep danger more than an arm's length away.

This same argument can be applied to medical treatment. I shall give an example that depends on modern knowledge of infection. Should the application of antibiotic ointment be allowed on the Sabbath if someone cuts his hand? It is a long step from cutting one's hand to being in danger of death, but infection is potentially life-threatening, and an argument could be made that minor cures should be allowed in order to be safe; conceivably, a small cut could become infected, and a minor wound might turn into a major illness. Ancient Jews did not know about bacteria and infection, and consequently causes and effects in medical matters were by no means clear to them. Some people had minor injuries or illnesses that escalated in ways that were not at all visible. Who knew which illness or injury would lead to death? Therefore, possibly cures of even minor problems should be allowed.

These examples are hypothetical, but the general point is not. Both the early rabbis and one wing of the Essene party discussed minor cures on the Sabbath;[13] if the most pious discussed this topic, it is highly probable that many ordinary Jews were willing to attempt to heal even minor injuries or illnesses on the Sabbath. They could have had an argument: "We do not know for sure which accidents or illnesses will turn out to be fatal."

This gives us, I hope, enough perspective to understand the Sabbath passages in the Gospels. Although not all of them bear on healing, those that do not nevertheless require us to understand the question of "mitigating circumstances": when is a problem serious enough to justify transgression of the Sabbath? There are several passages about the Sabbath in the Gospels, and I shall discuss the major ones.

Plucking Grain on the Sabbath (Matt 12:1-8; Mark 2:23-28; Luke 6:1-5). According to this passage, Jesus and his disciples were going through a grain field and were hungry. The disciples, not Jesus, picked grain and started to eat it. The Pharisees (who, quite surprisingly, were looking on) asked Jesus why he allowed his disciples to break the law. In Mark's version, Jesus appealed to the precedent of David, who, when he and his men were hungry, ate holy bread, ordinarily forbidden to laymen. The passage concludes with two sayings: "The Sabbath was made for man, not man for the Sabbath"; "The Son of man is lord of the Sabbath." According to Matthew, Jesus advanced still another argument: on the Sabbath the priests in the temple work (by sacrificing) but are considered innocent.

In this passage, Jesus argues that there were mitigating circumstances that excuse the violation: the disciples were hungry. A modern analogy to this argument would be defending driving over the speed limit by explaining that a passenger is ill. Moreover, Jesus offers a precedent (in Matthew, two precedents). This is like arguing that, previously, a driver who sped because of an emergency was not fined. Appealing to mitigating circumstances (hunger) and precedent (David) shows fundamental respect for the law. There is nothing in this passage to indicate that Jesus wished to oppose the Sabbath law. On the contrary, the implication is that he and his disciples ordinarily kept it. He was prepared to argue that a minor breach was justified by hunger, and for this argument he appealed to biblical precedent. It follows that he did not reject the Sabbath law as such.

The Man with the Withered Hand (Matt 12:9-14; Mark 3:1-6; Luke 6:6-11). In this story, Jesus heals a man on the Sabbath by telling him to stretch out his hand. Apparently he did no work;

talking is not work. Even in the strictest legal documents from first-century Judaism, the *Covenant of Damascus* and the Qumran *Community Rule*, there is no hint that talking on the Sabbath was regarded as a transgression. Moreover, we again note that Jesus offers an argument to justify his action: "Is it lawful on the Sabbath to do good or to do harm, to save life or to kill?" (Mark 3:6). This justification seems to imply that Jesus accepted the argument that was sketched above: One cannot know for sure when an apparently minor illness will lead to death; therefore, minor cures are permitted. We also note that, as in the previous case, Jesus' appeal to mitigating circumstances shows that he did not oppose the Sabbath law in principle. Thus, although (according to Mark) the scribes who looked on took grave exception to the cure of the man's hand, the reader of the passage cannot say that Jesus opposed the Sabbath law.

Further Passages in Luke. Luke contains two other passages that deserve comment: 13:10-17 and 14:1-6. According to the first, Jesus healed a woman on the Sabbath by laying his hands on her and telling her that she was healed. According to the second, he "took" a man and healed him on the Sabbath. "Taking" seems to mean that he put his hands on the man in connection with the healing. Both these cases probably would have been regarded as transgressions by members of the pietist parties. As we noted above, the early rabbis discussed minor cures on the Sabbath, and they generally regarded work done on these occasions as wrong. For example, in one case they discussed whether a person with a sore tooth could put vinegar on it. The answer was that this should not be done, but that the sufferer could eat something with vinegar on it, and thus avoid transgression.[14] We cannot know whether Galilean Pharisees in Jesus' day would have held the same opinion, but it is reasonable to assume that they would not have disagreed very much.

I think it probable that the most pious groups in Judaism in Jesus' day would either have opposed or looked askance at performing minor cures on the Sabbath if they required work. But the discussions in the *Covenant of Damascus* (presumably reflecting one wing of the Essene party) and Mishnah *Shabbat* (which stems from the rabbinic successors of the Pharisees) reveal, by their tone and content, that most Jews did not agree. The rabbis even disagreed among themselves about the status of minor cures. It is historically conceivable that Jesus performed one or more minor cures on the Sabbath by laying his hands on the injured or afflicted person, and that some pietists objected. This would not have been, however, a major issue; it was one about which reasonable people could agree to disagree. Some people would do no work on the Sabbath unless there was an obvious and immediate threat to life. Some took a more lenient view, and Jesus appears to have belonged to the latter group—which was, in all probability, a large one. It is most dubious that minor cures on the Sabbath were a major item of disagreement between Jesus and other pious Jews.

Jesus and Food Laws

Two major passages in the Hebrew Bible (Lev 11; Deut 14) prohibit various foods. The two most famous are pork and shellfish, but the exclusions also cover birds of prey, rodents, insects, donkeys, carnivorous animals, and numerous other potential foods—many of which have been and are as objectionable to non-Jews as to Jews. These laws were very important to first-century Jews, who clung to them despite the fact that Gentiles ridiculed them for avoiding the most succulent meat, pork. The significance of the food laws was in some ways much greater outside of Palestine than in Palestine. A Jew who lived in Jerusalem would have found it quite difficult to break the food laws. Pigs were not kept anywhere near Jerusalem, and the closest source of shellfish was many miles away. Apart from the problems of transporting forbidden foods to Jewish cities and villages in Palestine, moral suasion would have been very strong. The vendors and the consumers of pork or shellfish would both have been reported to the authorities, and the populace would have expressed its disfavor in very strong ways. There were, of course, gentile cities in geographical Galilee, and there it would be easy for a Palestinian Jew to disobey the food laws. Had he wished to flaunt these laws, Jesus could have gone to Scythopolis (for example), where pork surely could be had. As far as we know, he did not do this.

For Jews who lived in gentile surroundings (such as Paul), the issue was quite different. Pork was readily available (it was probably the most common meat), and shellfish could be obtained in any town that was close to the Mediterranean. In the gentile cities of Asia Minor and Greece, the markets, managed by civic officers, offered what the managers decreed. Some market managers were not especially friendly to Jews, but after the Jews aided Julius Caesar, he showed his appreciation in various ways, some direct and some indirect. One of the results was that the Greek-speaking cities of Asia Minor began passing decrees in favor of the Jews. Among the top three or four items was the right to have their own food.[15] The managers of the markets were forced to supply the Jews with their "ancestral food." It appears that previously the Jews did not always have food that Moses allowed. That is, in Palestine, nothing was easier than to observe the Mosaic food laws: they were hard to disobey. Outside Palestine, the situation was reversed: obedience to Moses sometimes left Jews in very grave difficulties. Some, no doubt, transgressed rather than go hungry. Julius Caesar corrected this situation, but we do not know how long this more favorable climate lasted.

It Is Not What Goes In (Matt 15:10-20; Mark 7:14-23).
According to Mark (7:1-8), Jesus fell into a dispute with some Pharisees and scribes about handwashing. This argument led to his pronouncement that "there is nothing outside a person which by going into him can defile, but the things which come out of a person are

what defile" (Mark 7:15). After the crowd departed, Jesus explained his view to the disciples: "Do you not see that whatever goes into a person from outside cannot defile him, since it enters, not his heart but his stomach, and so passes on?" (Mark 7:18-19). The author of the Gospel then adds: "Thus he declared all food clean."

If the author of Mark correctly states Jesus' own view, we have here an explicit statement that the law of Moses need not be observed. That is, if Jesus "declared all food clean," he opposed both Leviticus 11 and Deuteronomy 14. It is, however, dubious that the author's comment in Mark 7:19 reflects Jesus' own view. This is potentially a long argument, one that I have made in more detail elsewhere,[16] and I shall here merely outline the points.

1. The passage appears in both Matthew and Mark, but only Mark states that Jesus declared all foods clean. In Matthew, Jesus neither here nor elsewhere counsels his followers to break the law.

2. The saying in Mark 7:15 does not necessarily mean that Jesus intended to denounce the food laws. For the sake of emphasis, I shall quote it again: "There is nothing outside a person which by going into him can defile, but the things which come out of a person are what defile him." The construction *not . . . but* quite frequently means "not only this, but much more that."[17] When Moses told the Israelites that their murmurings were *not* against Aaron and himself, *but* against the Lord, they had just been complaining to *him* (Exod 16:2-8). The sentence means, "Your murmurings directed against us are in reality against the Lord, since we do his will." When the author of the *Epistle of Aristeas* wrote that Jews "honor God" *not* with gifts or sacrifices, *but* with purity of heart and of devout disposition" (*Ep. Arist.* 234), he did not mean that sacrifices were not brought, nor that he was against them (see, e.g., *Ep. Arist.* 170–71), but rather that what really matters is what they symbolize. Similarly, Mark 9:37, "Whoever receives me, receives *not* me *but* the one who sent me," means "receiving me is tantamount to receiving God." "*Not* what goes in *but* what comes out" in Mark 7:15, then,

probably means, "What comes out—the wickedness of a person's heart—is what really matters," leaving the food laws as such untouched. In this case there is no conflict with the law. This interpretation of the core saying in Mark 7:15 leads to the conclusion that the interpretation in 7:19 is incorrect.

3. After Jesus' death, his disciples did not know that he had told them to eat whatever food they liked. According to Acts 10, Peter three times saw a vision of all sorts of animals, including "beasts of prey and reptiles," and a voice told him, "kill and eat."[18] These foods were, of course, forbidden by Moses. Even after seeing this vision and hearing the commandment three times, Peter remained puzzled as to the meaning (Acts 10:17). Had Jesus already explained to his disciples that they could disregard the food laws (Mark 7:19), Peter would probably have understood the vision more quickly. Later, Peter and James disputed several points of the Jewish law with Paul—especially circumcision but also food laws and the Sabbath. It appears that neither side could appeal to the teaching of Jesus for support.[19] The conclusion to be drawn, then, is that Mark's statement in 7:19, "he declared all foods clean," represents a possible interpretation of Jesus' words, but not a necessary one. Moreover, the other early Christians did not think that Jesus had canceled the food laws for his followers.

Other Legal Issues

A complete treatment of Jesus and the first table of the Jewish law would include more topics: purity, tithes, other offerings, blasphemy, fasting, and worship. Scholars usually regard the three that we have considered (sacrifice, Sabbath, and food) as the major areas where Jesus may have opposed the law. I shall not here attempt to analyze these other topics in detail, partly because of the preferred length of these essays, partly because I have discussed all these issues elsewhere.[20] I shall instead make a few comments.

1. Purity. The major purity issue in the Gospels is leprosy. In a passage that we discussed under "sacrifice" (Mark 1:40-44), Jesus commands the leper to do what Moses commanded him; there is no opposition to the law.

Handwashing before meals (Mark 7:5) was a tradition followed by a few Jews, but it was not a law. The Hebrew Bible contains no commandment to wash hands before eating. In Jesus' day, some Jews probably washed their hands before eating, but some did not.[21]

2. Tithes, and so on. According to Matthew 23:23, Jesus agreed that even minor herbs should be tithed.

3. Fasting. The Hebrew Bible requires only one fast, on the Day of Atonement. There is no indication that Jesus feasted on this day. Various groups, and sometimes an entire city or region, might fast for some special reason: to commemorate a day of destruction, to try to persuade God to send rain, and so on. According to Mark 2:18-22, Jesus and his followers did not fast on some occasion when the Pharisees and the disciples of John the Baptist were fasting. This was obviously an optional fast, because only members of two pietist groups were observing it. The law of Moses was not in question.

4. Worship. The gospel evidence is that, on Sabbaths, Jesus attended the synagogue (e.g., Mark 1:21). Unfortunately, we are not told much about Jesus' worship in the temple. We do know, however, that he observed at least one festival, which included eating an animal sacrificed in the temple (e.g., Mark 14:12). The Gospels omit most of the details of Jesus' life prior to his short ministry, and I assume that he had previously attended the temple during one or more festivals each year. In any case, there is no evidence that he refused to worship the God of Israel in the way that the Hebrew Bible commands.

5. Blasphemy. This is potentially a major issue; according to the trial scenes in the synoptic gospels, Jesus was accused of and executed for blasphemy. I hope that readers who accept this view will

take the time to study my earlier discussions.[22] In brief, the situation is this: According to Mark, the high priest cried, "Blasphemy!" when Jesus admitted that he was "the Christ, the Son of the Blessed" (Mark 14:61-64). According to Matthew and Luke, he did not give a clear answer. But we may stay with Mark. As the author presents the account, the high priest was determined to have Jesus executed. His first effort was to have Jesus accused of attacking the temple (Mark 14:55-60). This charge was thrown out. He then got Jesus to admit that he was "the son of the Blessed," and immediately cried "Blasphemy!" There is nothing intrinsically blasphemous in the claim to be son of God. All ancient Jews thought of themselves as sons of God. What we learn from this passage is *not* that Jesus held blasphemous views of himself (that he put himself on the same level as God), but that the high priest would take any admission as an excuse for the verdict that he desired. That is, the high priest had determined that Jesus should die. The question of the charge was only technical. If a group of Jewish legal authorities, either past or present, coolly examined what Jesus said (or is reported to have said), they would not conclude that he was a blasphemer.

CONCLUSION

Many Christians believe that Jesus opposed his native religion. If so, he should have spoken against either its theology or its ethics—that is, against the table of laws that govern relations between humans and God or those that apply to humans' relations with other humans. I cannot find the evidence that he attacked either table. His debates and arguments with his contemporaries fall within the parameters of disagreement in his place and time. With regard to his view of the laws on the first table, with which this essay concerns itself, we cannot say that Jesus was against monotheism, sacrifice, the Sabbath, or food laws. I have more briefly sketched other possible topics of disagreement. We find that Jesus did not oppose the laws of purity, of support of the priesthood, of fasting, or of worship. We have also seen that he did not denigrate or blaspheme against God.

This does not mean that he did not have his own distinctive viewpoints. On the contrary, it is plain that he did so. (I have not discussed them in this essay.) I can well imagine that he rubbed some people the wrong way. Joseph Caiaphas, the high priest, clearly thought that Jesus should be done away with. But that was not because he and Jesus disagreed about Deuteronomy or Leviticus. I have elsewhere argued extensively that Caiaphas was afraid of civil turmoil and that Jesus posed a threat to peace and order. To understand the death of Jesus, we would have to change topics and discuss the politics of the day. With regard to our present subject, however, we should conclude that Jesus did not favor transgression of the laws on the first table of the law of Moses.

For Discussion

1. State and explain the two tables of the law found in Judaism.

2. How did Jesus relate to the two tables of the law? Are there any passages in the Gospels that indicate Jesus' view of the law?

3. How is the term "love" as used in the passages quoted in this essay from Leviticus, Deuteronomy, Philo, the Talmud, Tobit, and the Gospels to be understood?

4. In the second commandment: "You shall not bow down to [idols] or serve them" (Deut 5:9), how should the word "serve" be understood in light of Judaism and other ancient religions?

5. What was Jesus' attitude toward sacrifice? Were his views similar to or the same as those held by other Jewish thinkers and teachers?

6. When did the Sabbath become an important and distinctive feature of Jewish life? What activities are prohibited on the Sabbath and is this a matter of interpretation? When is a problem serious enough to justify transgression of the Sabbath?

7. From the Gospel texts dealing with the Sabbath that are analyzed in this chapter, how would you explain Jesus' attitude toward and behavior on the Sabbath?

8. What was Jesus' attitude toward food laws? How does Jesus' saying in Mark 7:14-23, especially verses 18 and 19a affect your understanding of his approach to food laws?

9. Summarize Jesus' approaches to laws surrounding purity, tithing, fasting, worship, and blasphemy. How different is his approach from those of his contemporaries?

10. From reading this chapter, how have your attitudes and understandings about Jesus' approach to his native religion changed or been improved?

PART THREE

FROM JESUS TO CHRIST

5

FROM JESUS TO CHRIST: THE CONTRIBUTION OF THE APOSTLE PAUL

PAULA FREDRIKSEN

The transformation of Jesus of Nazareth, the historical figure, into Christ, the subject of revelation and object of faith and hope, takes place during the prehistoric period of Christianity. By "prehistoric" I mean before the written record. In this essay, I investigate the growth of this new religious movement during those decades between the resurrection of Jesus and our earliest documented interpretation of it, namely, the letters of Paul. In that relatively brief time—between, let us say, 30 C.E. and 50 C.E.—this Jewish messianic movement had crossed several important frontiers. It had moved from Aramaic, the primary language of its rural Galilean phase, to the flexible *koine* Greek spoken throughout the Eastern Mediterranean. It had moved out from its native Jewish homeland to the cities of the Western Diaspora. And, on the evidence of Paul, it had crossed a crucial ethnic and cultural frontier, from being primarily a Jewish movement to a movement made up largely of Gentiles.[1]

Our best evidence for reconstructing these lost decades at the dawn of Christianity is preserved in the New Testament. An anthology of late first- and early second-century texts collected and definitively canonized only in the fourth century, the New Testament contains no firsthand eyewitness accounts of the life and teachings of Jesus.[2] For our purposes, what matters most is not what Jesus himself might have thought or taught during his lifetime, but the claims made about him after his death, namely, that he had been raised, and that this fact had universal significance for humankind. And to this message, Paul, not the evangelists, is our earliest witness.

Scholarly consensus takes seven of the fourteen canonical letters attributed to Paul as authentic: 1 Thessalonians, 1 and 2 Corinthians, Philippians, Philemon, Galatians, and Romans.[3] Paul states clearly that he had never known Jesus "according to the flesh," but he at least knew others who had, and he was in some kind of collegial contact with them—Peter, John, and James, to name a few. Earlier by a good fifteen years than our next earliest evidence, Mark's Gospel, Paul's letters are nonetheless some twenty years late in terms of the period of Jesus' activity. If all we had were Paul's letters and for some reason lacked the Gospels, we would know almost nothing about Jesus—not where he was from or what he did, and very little of what he said.[4] The human figure of Jesus does not concern Paul; the focus of his attention and commitment is the risen Christ.

Paul met the risen Christ at a moment that scholars refer to as his "conversion," although Paul thinks of it as his "call"—a call specifically to be God's *apostolos*, or messenger, to the Gentiles. He spends very little time in his extant correspondence describing either this figure, the risen Christ, or his experience of him. In fact, all we have securely is two clauses in two different letters. In Galatians, he says, "When he who had set me apart before I was born

78

and had called me through his grace was pleased to reveal his son to me in order that I might preach him among the Gentiles . . ." and then the sentence goes on, concluding on the point that Paul was at least the equal of those who had preceded him in the Jesus movement (Gal 1:15-17). In 1 Corinthians 15, Paul passes on a tradition he has about the sequence of Christ's postresurrection appearances: first to Peter (Cephas), then to "the twelve," then to 500 brethren, then to James, then to all the apostles. "Last of all, as to one untimely born, he appeared also to me" (1 Cor 15:1-8). Last, but not least—certainly not, in Paul's own opinion. "[God's] grace toward me has not been in vain. On the contrary, I work harder than any of them"—that is, than his colleagues in the movement. This is pure Paul.

So Christ, not Jesus, is at the heart of Paul's proclamation. What does he say about this figure? As John Donahue points out (chap. 6), Paul uses the term "Christ"—the Greek translation of the Hebrew *Messiah*—without ever unpacking what he means by it or why he confers it on Jesus. Why on earth a Jew who had been crucified and then raised should be designated *Messiah* by another first-century Jew who obviously knew his scriptures is a question scholars have had a hard time answering. Paul uses the title "Christ"—*christos*—virtually as Jesus' last name, and except for one brief clause as he opens his letter to the Romans—"descended from David according to the flesh" (1:4)—Paul nowhere tells us what he means by "Christ."

Paul, rather, describes the *function* of this figure, whom he also refers to as "Lord" and "Son." This figure *"died for our sins* in accordance with the scriptures" (1 Cor 15:3), but Paul does not reveal what scriptures support his claim. He would have had difficulty finding anything about a crucified messiah in the Hebrew Scriptures (Old Testament). But Paul's main point about this Christ is not so much that he was crucified as that *he was raised* and that *he is about to come back*. Paul, further, felt compelled by his reception of this message to preach Christ *to the Gentiles,* and we must infer from his frequent recourse to scripture when he writes to his communities that these Gentiles were not ignorant of the idea of Israel and of God's election of Israel as expressed in the scriptures. Paul may be taking his message to Gentiles, but these are Gentiles *who also have some knowledge of the Bible* (Hebrew Scripture).

Bear these linked facts in mind as we proceed: Paul believed Jesus to be raised and to be about to return; he proclaimed this good news to Gentiles, and these Gentiles were themselves in some degree familiar with the biblical promises to Israel. Paul, further, continued to regard himself as a Jew—"a Hebrew born of Hebrews" (Phil 3:5) and one of the elect of Israel (Rom 11:2, 7)—and he constructed his mission and message entirely within Judaism.[5] We know that this movement would eventually become independent of Judaism and even hostile to it; but nothing would have surprised Paul, his other Jewish colleagues in the movement, and even his Gentiles in Christ, more. These new communities were called by Paul and by others[6] into the redemptive history of Israel, although *they were not thereby converted to Judaism.* As we see how this was so, as we reconstruct the prehistory of Christianity, we shall reconstruct as well the transformation of Jesus into Christ.

Let us consider, for the moment, not ideas so much as social reality. Who are the people we are investigating—Jews and Gentiles—and how did they regard each other? Jews were a minority in the Roman Empire; particularly Jews who lived in the Diaspora, in and among Gentiles, had plenty of time to contemplate gentile culture and the sort of people it produced. What did they think? Here is one mid-first-century opinion from a Greek-speaking, well-traveled Jew. I translate loosely:

> Gentiles do not know God; or, rather, they see him through creation but then do not honor him nor give him thanks. Instead, they exchange the glory of the immortal God for images of mortal man, or of birds, animals, and even reptiles. They are, consequently, impure in

the lusts of their heart. They worship the creature rather than the Creator and for that reason God has handed them over to their own dishonorable passions. The women are sexually perverse; the men lust after one another. Their minds are base and their conduct indecent. They are filled with all manner of wickedness, evil, covetousness and malice. They are full of envy, murder, strife, deceit, malignity. They gossip and they slander. They hate God. They are insolent, haughty, boastful, inventors of evil, disobedient to parents. Foolish. Faithless. Heartless. Ruthless.

Paul vents this opinion in chapter 1 of Romans. Gentile culture—the only option to Jewish culture in the mid-first century—perceived as perverse religiously and therefore socially, expressed its spiritual perversion particularly, in Jewish eyes, in sexual misconduct.[7] We've just heard what Paul thinks of this sort of thing. Why and how, then, does he spend time with such people?

The abstract middle distance separating Gentiles from Jews in this sort of cultural polemic disappears in the real environment of the Mediterranean city.[8] Both social and religious reality conspired to bring these groups into close contact. Jews in the Diaspora organized their community life around the synagogue, and Gentiles, ecumenical to a fault,[9] evidently felt free to visit these if they so chose. Synagogues attracted interested outsiders, and Jews did not discourage outside sympathy. We have a range of evidence from antiquity attesting to a gentile penumbra around diaspora synagogues, within which we find grades of interest and affiliation, from mild curiosity to the threshold of conversion.

Philo of Alexandria, for example, an elder contemporary of Jesus and Paul, mentions the "multitudes of others" who joined with Egyptian Jews in their annual celebration of the miracle of the Torah's translation from Hebrew to Greek, "to thank God for the good gift so old yet ever new."[10] Others, as the Greek magical papyri perhaps evince, might attend synagogue services out of professional interest, to acquire knowledge of a powerful god in whose name they could command demons.[11] Philo and especially Josephus, the historian of the Jewish war against Rome, claim that judaizers—pagans voluntarily attached to the synagogue and interested in Jewish religious practice—could be found in numbers in urban centers throughout the Empire.[12] Hostile gentile witnesses also report the same: Horace, Juvenal, and, later, Tacitus all comment without enthusiasm on this gentile habit of judaizing.[13]

Pagans could judaize without making an exclusive commitment to the religion of Israel. Luke, for example, both in his Gospel and in the book of Acts, mentions such Gentiles who on the one hand voluntarily assume aspects of Jewish piety but, nonetheless, remain public pagans, worshiping traditional gods. Thus the centurion at Capernaum who "loves our nation [Israel] and built us our synagogue" (Luke 7:1-10), whether fictive or not, would have been understood by Luke's ancient audience to be a practicing pagan, responsible for performing the cult that would have attended his military unit. So too the centurion Cornelius in Acts 10, "a devout man who feared God . . . gave alms . . . and prayed constantly . . . well-spoken by the whole Jewish nation" (10:2, 22). A third-century inscription from Aphrodisias in Turkey preserves an index of Jewish–Gentile interaction. It lists Jews, names members of a prayer or study group, designates converts as such (*proselytoi*), and separately lists fifty-four *theosebeis*—pagan Godfearers. Nine of these are likewise given as members of the city council, and thus responsible for the sacrifices to the gods (of the city and of the empire) that were incumbent on a town official.[14] Later Christian writers—in the second, third, and fourth centuries—complain about the synagogue's toleration of Gentiles, both pagan and Christian. Apparently, this gentile habit of judaizing continued even after conversion to Christianity.[15]

The point of our overview is that Gentiles could be both practicing pagans and public affiliates of the Jewish community. Further, although the synagogue allowed gentile adherents, it did not demand that Gentiles relinquish their own traditional religions. Gentiles' allegiance to Judaism was various, idiosyncratic, and completely voluntary. They remained pagan, but, through the synagogue, where Moses was "read every Sabbath" (Acts 15:21), such Gentiles would have acquired some knowledge of the Bible. It was among Gentiles such as these, I believe, that Paul built up the *ekklesia tou Christou*, his communities in Christ.

How would the Bible have provided both Paul and his gentile audience with a religious framework for understanding the purpose and meaning of their new community? Here we have to consider the biblical story of God and Israel, and the ways that Gentiles figure into that relationship.

Genesis begins with God's creative action. Only God is god. He makes everything that is, the whole universe and all people. As the story unwinds, it establishes a moral resonance between the Creator—just, kind, merciful—and his particular creature, made uniquely in his image. Humanity generally, and Israel in particular, must acknowledge a certain divinely established standard of religious and ethical behavior.[16] This moral dynamic presupposes that God, who acts in and through history for the benefit of his creation, is neither arbitrary nor perverse. He has an investment in human society and history, and will not indefinitely countenance the hegemony of evil. Ultimately, he will see that good prevails.

The God of the Bible is the author of a divine comedy in which good *will* win out in the end. This is a normative view within Judaism to this day, expressed in synagogue prayer service in the *Amidah*[17] and the *Alenu*,[18] and anticipated in the traditional grace said after meals. This same theme, set within a dramatically foreshortened time frame, likewise defines biblical *apocalyptic eschatology*, the expectation that God will realize final redemption *soon*. Apocalyptic eschatology as a religious sensibility describes an arc that passes through the later books of the classical prophets of the Jewish canon—Isaiah, Jeremiah, Ezekiel, Daniel,[19] the twelve minor prophets—through the letters of Paul, certain evangelical passages, and finally the book of Revelation, which closes the Christian canon. Along this arc, we can plot the convictions of John the Baptist, the Qumran sectarians, Jesus of Nazareth, and Paul himself.

Apocalyptic eschatology presents a vision of salvation in a historical idiom: its images are profoundly inspired by the experience of the Babylonian captivity.[20] Redemption is imaged concretely: not only from sin or evil, but from exile. The twelve tribes are restored (ten, remember, had been missing since the Assyrian conquest of the North in 722 B.C.E.), the people are gathered back to the land, the temple and Jerusalem are renewed and made splendid, a pure priesthood is established, the Davidic monarchy is restored. Social justice and true religion prevail, as God's lordship is universally acknowledged.

As apocalyptic literature develops and flourishes in the period between, roughly, the Maccabees and the Mishnah, 200 B.C.E. to 200 C.E., we find emphases on various combinations of traditional themes. Typically, we might find a battle between Good and Evil just before the End. Sometimes a messiah leads the battle; sometimes an archangel; sometimes God himself. The *War Scroll*, from Qumran, expects two messiahs, one priestly and one military; the *Assumption of Moses*, a pseudepigraphical text, none; later Christian texts, a messiah who comes twice, his more military role relegated to his second coming. Terrestial and celestial disturbances signal the onset of the End of the Age: eclipses, falling stars, earthquake, famine, plague, war.[21] We might find a resurrection of the dead, or perhaps of only the righteous dead, and some kind of judgment. God reveals himself in glory; he vanquishes evil and pours his spirit out upon the people; he establishes Peace.

Where are the Gentiles in this picture? Different texts present different views, and frequently one text, like Isaiah, presents many views. Wicked Gentiles, particularly those who had persecuted Israel, are destroyed or are led captive to Jerusalem. Foreign monarchs lick the dust at Israel's feet (Isa 49:23; cf. Mic 7:16-17); gentile cities are devastated, to be repopulated by Israel (Isa 54:3; Zeph 2:1–3:8); God destroys the nations and their idols (Mic 5:9, 15). Yet this literature also anticipates gentile inclusion in redemption. The nations gather together with Israel to worship God in his temple (Isa 2:2-4); on God's mountain, the temple mount, they feast together on the meal God has prepared for them (Isa 25:6). Gentiles will shake off their idols and accompany Jews on their homeward journey. Here is one of my favorite passages, from Zechariah:

> Thus says the Lord of hosts: Peoples shall yet come, even the inhabitants of many cities. The inhabitants of one city will go to another, saying: "Let us go at once to entreat the favor of the Lord, and to seek the Lord of hosts; I am going." Many peoples and strong nations shall come and seek the Lord of hosts in Jerusalem, and to entreat the favor of the Lord. . . . In those days ten men from the nations of every tongue shall take hold of the robe of a Jew, saying, "Let us go with you, for we have heard that God is with you." (Zech 8:20-23)

At the End, the nations (in Hebrew, *goyim*) will turn to God. Jewish apocalyptic hope, in other words, anticipates a *double* redemption: Israel (both the living and the dead) returns from exile, and the Gentiles turn from idolatry. Note, though, that the nations do not thereby *become* Jews. This is not a story about universal religious conversion in that sense: the texts still speak of the nations *as* Gentiles. These Gentiles, however, experience a *moral* conversion, *from* the worship of idols *to* the worship of "the God of Jacob."

Some Jews thus expected the Kingdom of God to be ethnically diverse. His people would comprise at least two nations: Israel, and everybody else (e.g., Zech 2:11; also, as we will see momentarily, Rom 11). Much like the diaspora synagogues in normal time, God's kingdom at the end of time would encompass both Jews and Gentiles. But the apocalyptic scenario anticipates a religious reorientation that the quotidian synagogue neither expected nor demanded:

Eschatological Gentiles, unlike their quotidian counterparts, will have renounced their traditional gods. Once the Lord of the universe had revealed himself in glory, how could they do otherwise?[22] The social reality of diaspora Godfearers and this religious tradition of eschatological Gentiles together provide the explanatory context for Paul's (and other Jewish apostles') policy toward Gentiles "in Christ." *Paul demands of his Gentiles something the synagogue never did:* They absolutely *must* relinquish their idols. His unambiguous demand gives us the measure of his absolute conviction that he lived at the end of the age, at the cusp of the great transformation anticipated by Jewish tradition.[23] With the resurrection of Christ, the end of the age *had already come* (1 Cor 10:11). True, Christ had to return to sum things up, to clearly and once-for-all defeat evil and even death itself (1 Cor 15); but in the meantime, those baptized into Christ's resurrection—namely, Paul's Gentiles—along with the believing remnant of Israel, lived in a wrinkle in time. And if, by participating in Christ's death and resurrection through baptism, these Gentiles were in some sense proleptically in the Kingdom, there was no room for idols—or social indifference, or sexual sin—any more.

There was no tradition in antiquity that Gentiles affiliated with the synagogue should give up their traditional religious practices. Only in the instance of *conversion*—that is, becoming a Jew and therefore assuming responsibility for the divinely revealed *mitzvot* of the Torah—was such a demand made. For male converts, this entailed circumcision as well.[24] Evidently, by mid-century (c. 49 C.E.), some other Jewish apostles within the Jesus movement—made anxious, perhaps, by the continuing delay of Christ's return and the intrinsically unstable situation of affiliated but nonintegrated Gentiles in their new communities—began to press for full conversion to Judaism, that is, circumcision for men. Paul, as we know from his report of this situation in his letter to the Galatians, condemned this position; so did James, Peter, and John (Gal 2:1-10). Traditional biblical expectation held against this innovation—preaching Judaism to Gentiles[25]—that the "circumcision party" had improvised. For Gentiles to participate in the Kingdom, the other apostles held, relinquishing idols would suffice.

Paul expected this awkward stage between the resurrection and the Parousia to be brief—coincident, perhaps, with the duration of his own mission—and many of his comments give us his gauge. His earliest letter, 1 Thessalonians, reveals that his community there had expected Christ's return so shortly that they were troubled by the unanticipated deaths of some community members: Would they thus not participate in redemption? Paul writes to assure them that they would (4:13-18; 5:9-10). 1 Corinthians 11:30 refers to a similar situation—Christian Gentiles dying before the return of Christ. Paul suggests there that such deaths might be punitive, hence exceptional. Elsewhere in 1 Corinthians, he states that "the form of this world is passing away" (7:31); so close is the "impending distress" (the travails before the Endtime? 7:26) that Paul can reasonably suggest that his Gentiles refrain from sexual intercourse and devote themselves to prayer (7:1-7, 25-31). Repeated references to the "day of Christ" in Philippians[26] culminate in his assertion, "The Lord is at hand" (4:4). In view of "what hour it is"—how soon before final redemption—Christians should pay taxes and avoid tangling with the government (Rom 13:1-12). "The God of peace will soon crush Satan under your feet" (16:20).

The resurrection of Jesus, experienced by those who had originally followed him and also by Paul (1 Cor 15), had plunged his earliest apostles into the charged expectation of imminent redemption. But as the time lengthened between Jesus' resurrection and the coming Kingdom, these apostles had to revise the traditional scenario, which had presented resurrection as a communal Endtime event.[27] Jesus' resurrection, reinterpreted, was seen as the sign and surety of the general resurrection, and transformation of reality, about to come.[28] In the interim, these apostles felt called to take the good news of the coming Kingdom—now linked to Jesus' second, glorious coming—to the rest of Israel: Judea, Samaria, back to Galilee, thence to the synagogues of the Diaspora,[29] where Gentiles, too, would be encountered in numbers. Hence the ready and early inclusion of Gentiles in the Jesus movement: Jewish tradition had long anticipated their participation in eschatological redemption. We still feel the sweep of this stage of the early movement, the energy and confidence of its revision of Jesus' message of the Kingdom,[30] when we read Paul's letters.

But these letters are late. By the time we have them, we also have another major revision, this one Paul's own. We see it most clearly in his final letter, to the Romans. But here we must exercise historical imagination, and not be fooled by the distance—cultural and chronological—that stretches between us and Paul. To us, in the perspective of twenty centuries, any ancient evidence coming from within twenty years of Jesus' execution may look comfortably close to originating events. But try to imagine things from Paul's perspective. By the time he composed the letters that remain in our canon, he had been a member of a movement that had been preaching the imminent return of the Lord and the coming of the Kingdom *for almost a generation*. Not only had the Kingdom not come, but, as time passed, fewer and fewer within Israel were finding this message of a crucified and coming messiah credible.

Time drags when you expect it to end. How had Paul managed, despite the counterevidence of his own experience, to assert with conviction right to the end that the Endtime was on the way? How could he be so certain, after two decades of preaching this message, that "salvation is *nearer* to us than when we first believed" (Rom 13:11)?

The answer, again, lies with his Gentiles. Think back to his social context, to his scathing opinion of gentile society in Romans 1, which I quoted above. Now recall what he thinks he can reasonably demand of *his* Gentiles: No more fornication (1 Cor 5:1-2, 11; 7:2).

Forget about going to prostitutes (1 Cor 6:15-20). Sexual modesty should be observed even within marriage (1 Thess 4:4 RSV). Communities should have their own law courts (1 Cor 6:1-6; cf. 2 Cor 13:1). The community as a whole is responsible for widows, orphans, and the poor, both at home and in Jerusalem (1 Cor 11:17-22; 16:1-3; Rom 16:1-3; Gal 2:10). Absolutely and unequivocably abandon idols (1 Cor 5:11). Be slaves to righteousness (Rom 6:18). One can fulfill the Law without circumcision (Rom 2:14-16, 26-29).

Given Paul's estimate of the sort of person produced by gentile culture, it would take a miracle for his Gentiles to act the way that he insists they do. And that, in Paul's estimate, is exactly what it was: the degree to which they met his demands was the degree to which they were enabled by God's Spirit, given them through the death of his Son, in baptism (e.g., Rom 6:3-18, 22). In other words, the success of the Christian mission in turning these pagans into eschatological Gentiles who kept to a religious and moral standard never required of them by any synagogue, was proof for Paul that, through the Spirit, humanity had crossed the threshold into the next age. This gentile transformation justified Paul's religious convictions *as a Jew* that, in the death and resurrection of Jesus, God had begun the final transformation of the world, as he had promised Israel long ago: "For I tell you that Christ became a servant to the circumcised to show God's truthfulness, in order to confirm the promises given to the patriarchs, and in order that the Gentiles might glorify God for his mercy" (Rom 15:8-9).

The first Christian revision of the traditional prophetic scenario had been the interpolation of a missionary stage between Jesus' resurrection and his Parousia, his Second Coming.[31] The second revision, Paul's own, reordered the sequence of saved populations. Traditionally, Gentiles were to be the beneficiary of Israel's redemption. In Paul's view—the product of his experience, his unshakable confidence in his own convictions, and the facts of the Christian mission mid-century—Israel's redemption would follow

from the Gentiles'. This is the scheme he works out in Romans 9–
11. Now God has chosen only a remnant within Israel, such as Paul,
but the rest he has divinely hardened so that the gospel can go next
to the Gentiles. When the "full number" (*pleroma*) of Gentiles has
come in, then God will cease hardening Israel. At that point, all
Israel, and indeed all humanity, will be saved. "For God has con-
signed all men to disobedience, that he may have mercy upon all"
(Rom 11:32).

The Endtime, I note, is upon me too: I shall sum up. Whatever
constituted his experience of the risen Christ sometime around the
year 30 C.E., it was the moral and religious transformation of his
gentile communities in the following decades that confirmed Paul in
his conviction that, through the death and resurrection of Jesus, the
End really was at hand. This conviction articulates the profoundly
optimistic, profoundly Jewish commitment to a God who works redemption within history, for the benefit of his entire creation. And
it is this message, the message of biblical religion itself, that despite
the gaps yawning between them unites Jesus, the charismatic
prophet from Nazareth, to Paul, the apostle of the risen Christ.

For Discussion

1. Why was Paul not concerned with the human figure of Jesus,
   but rather with the risen Christ?

2. How did Paul use the term "Christ" in relation to Jesus? Did
   Paul tell his audience or subsequent readers what he means by
   the term "Christ"?

3. What is the function of the figure "Christ" whom Paul also
   refers to as "Lord" and "Son"?

4. Did Paul continue to regard himself as a Jew even after his
   "conversion" to the Jesus movement?

5. What was the relationship between Jews and Gentiles in the ancient world at the time of Paul? How does this relationship shed light on Paul's practice of preaching to and working with the Gentiles?

6. How would the Bible have provided a base for both Paul and his gentile audience for developing various "communities in Christ"?

7. What role does the apocalyptic literature and its understanding of eschatology play in the early inclusion of Gentiles into the Jesus movement?

8. What is it that Paul demands of his Gentiles that the synagogue never demanded? What is the significance of his demand for Gentiles to participate in the kingdom?

9. How does the gentile transformation confirm Paul in his conviction that, through the death and resurrection of Jesus, the Endtime was at hand?

10. From this chapter, what new understandings and insights do you have about Paul, the Gentiles, and the movement from Jesus to Christ?

6

FROM CRUCIFIED MESSIAH TO RISEN CHRIST: THE TRIAL OF JESUS REVISITED

JOHN R. DONAHUE, S.J.

◼

Very few sections of the Gospels have caused as much pain to the Jewish people and pose as great a challenge to dialogue between Christians and Jews as the narratives of the so-called trial of Jesus before Jewish authorities (Matt 26:57-68; Mark 14:53-65; Luke 22:54-71; John 11:47-53; 18:13-24 NSRV).[1] Gerald Sloyan, who has worked for decades in Jewish–Christian dialogue, calls the trial of Jesus and the "guilt question" thereby involved "the neuralgic point for Jewish and Christian relations over the centuries."[2] A naive and harmonized reading, which dominated Christian thought for centuries, would be somewhat as follows:

> After his betrayal and arrest, Jesus of Nazareth was tried by the highest Jewish court, the Sanhedrin, which found him guilty of blasphemy because of his claim to be God's Son. Because the Jewish

93

*officials did not have the right to execute him according to Jewish law,
they brought him before Pilate on a trumped-up charge of claiming to
be king. Pilate was the dupe of Jewish malice and ordered Jesus to be
crucified.*

After almost two centuries of historical criticism of the traditions
behind the Gospels, of investigation into the historical context of
Jesus' ministry, and of redaction and composition criticism of the
theological motivations at work in the formation of the Gospel narratives, virtually no element of this naive reading remains unchal-
lenged. In the present essay, I will survey some current scholarship
on the situation that led to the death of Jesus of Nazareth (and
which renders the naive view obsolete) and then suggest, albeit very
briefly, the path by which Jesus, the crucified Messiah, was proclaimed as the risen Christ by the early church. There has been an
explosion of important studies in both these areas, and there is
much contemporary ferment in research on the historical Jesus. It is
impossible, therefore, in this relatively short space, to give an adequate treatment to the complex issues involved.[3] My aim also is to
raise certain questions and to tender certain hypotheses for the sake
of discussion, rather than to offer fixed opinions.

REVIEWING THE TRIAL NARRATIVE

In 1973, in an initial study of the "trial" of Jesus before Jewish leaders as narrated in the Gospel of Mark, I argued, using the methods
of redaction and composition criticism, that, in 14:53-65, Mark had
constructed an elaborate scene of the trial of Jesus not to record historically what actually happened, but as part of a carefully orches-
trated presentation of major theological motifs of his Gospel,
principally, Christology or the identity of Jesus, the relation of Jesus
to the temple, and the challenge to Christian disciples.[4] At the end
of that work, I noted that the trial narrative of Mark is a dubious
source for the historical events surrounding the death of Jesus, and

cited the late Samuel Sandmel's stark statement that he had simply given up on trying to solve the problem of the historical events undergirding the theology.[5] My reservations about the historicity of the trial narrative were hardly original; by the 1970s, it had already been widely questioned.[6]

In the same year, Donald Juel, who has subsequently done so much to enhance our knowledge of the earliest Christological affirmations in the New Testament, completed his Yale dissertation, subsequently published as *Messiah and Temple*.[7] Juel argued cogently that the trial narrative was not primarily history, but "the place chosen by the author [Mark] to introduce themes of particular importance in the account of Jesus' death which follows."[8] Also in 1973, Gerald Sloyan of Temple University published a small but very important volume, *Jesus on Trial*, in which he argues cogently that the gospel narratives are heavily influenced by apologetic and theological concerns.[9] He concludes his study by stating:

> The man Jesus was dispatched in quite unusual circumstances in an age given to violence. We should not shrink from the harsh realities that attended to this particular reality. What exactly they were is hard to discover. Only a small portion of the data is recoverable.[10]

Subsequent studies of the trial and death of Jesus have not shaken the view that the gospel narratives are not motivated primarily by historical concerns but reflect the theology of the different Evangelists and the issues that were alive in their communities during the closing decades of the first century.[11] Recent research has turned again to historical issues surrounding the death of Jesus— with the realization, however, that the historical situation is more complex than was thought twenty years ago. In debt principally to the works of Raymond E. Brown, Martin Goodman, James McLaren, and E. P. Sanders, I will try to summarize some of the salient points of this research.[12]

The Status of the Sanhedrin

A virtual consensus of much early discussion, even by Jewish and Christian scholars who did not hold as factual a formal trial of Jesus before the Sanhedrin, was that there was a "supreme court" or council of Jews that met in Jerusalem under the leadership of the high priest. T. A. Burkill's description of the Sanhedrin is representative:

> The supreme Jewish Council of seventy-one members in Jerusalem during postexilic times; or one of the lower tribunals of twenty-three members of which Jerusalem had two. . . . The supreme court had legislative and executive, as well as judiciary, functions, but the extent of its effective authority varied considerably under different political regimes.[13]

Jewish writings, especially the tractates *Sanhedrin* in the Mishnah and Tosepta, provided the principal sources for such a view.

Contemporary historical studies challenge seriously this picture, principally for the following reasons. There is a growing realization that the legal prescriptions of the Tannaitic literature (Mishnah and Tosefta) do not reflect *actual practices and existing institutions* of the first century of the Common Era. Also, as E. P. Sanders, among others, has stressed, the Mishnah does not deal with a series of rules or laws that actually governed society, but often speaks of ideals, and its genre is a series of academic debates.[14] Sanders calls the Sanhedrin as depicted in these sources "a mythical source" of government.[15] James McLaren, a student of Sanders, examines twenty-one test cases of political and juridical actions in Flavius Josephus. His first conclusion is that "we have sufficient information to state that there was a formal institution in Jerusalem during the first century A.D. known as the *boulē*" which acquired the character of a national institution and which discussed issues pertinent to the city of Jerusalem.[16] This is *not* the Sanhedrin mentioned in Tannaitic or Christian texts, but rather a consultative body, most likely made up of people of wealth and influence, similar to local councils present in other Hellenistic cities. His second major conclusion is that there were two further institutions described by the same Greek term, *synedrion*, which were not standing institutions but functioned only for specific tasks, either consultative, where a Roman official called on specific Jewish groups to assist in determining a course of action, or judicial, a place of arbitration, a court, which was convened usually by a leading official such as the serving high priest.[17] Capital cases could be tried in this second type of *synedrion*. The relevance of this research to questions of the trial of Jesus is that Jesus would not have been tried by a Jewish "supreme court," conceived of as an ongoing institution made up of the major Jewish religious groups, but by a judicial *synedrion*, a more informal body convened most likely for his case. This *synedrion* was not the "Great Sanhedrin" of the Mishnah. The often stated view that the Jewish officials violated their own laws in the condemnation of Jesus has no validity, therefore; neither the Great Sanhedrin itself nor the rules of procedure outlined in the tractate *Sanhedrin* reflect first-century practice.[18]

The Governance of Judea in the First Century C.E.

A second area of important recent historical research touches on the actual governance of Judea during the first half of the first century C.E., specifically on relations between the principal Jewish authorities and the Roman prefect of Judea.[19] The last, tumultuous years of Herod the Great's reign (37–4 B.C.E.) were marked by domestic strife, interfamilial murder, and protests against his reign; his death was followed by various forms of unrest.[20] During Herod's last illness, two Jewish *sophistai*, whom Josephus calls "experts in the laws of their country," incited followers to tear down the golden eagle from the gate of the Herodian temple. Herod retaliated by ordering them to be burned alive.[21]

Herod was succeeded in Judea by his eldest son Archeleus, whom Joseph Fitzmyer describes as "the least liked of Herod's sons." Archeleus was known for his autocratic and at times brutal ways, shown in the arbitrary deposition of high priests.[22] During this period, throughout Judea, Galilee, and Perea, a series of popular revolts broke out which Richard Horsley characterizes as "popular messianic uprisings."[23] With some difficulty, these were suppressed by Varus, the legate of Syria, who, according to Josephus, crucified 2,000 Jews whom he held responsible for the revolt.[24] For nine troubled years, Archeleus maintained tenuous rule until he was deposed by the emperor Augustus (27 B.C.E.–14 C.E.) in 6 C.E., most likely at the urging of a delegation of Jews and Samaritans. At this time, Judea became a Roman equestrian province (the lowest of the three grades of Roman provinces). Often, the members of the equestrian order, which was based principally on wealth, were untrained and incompetent. Coponius, a Roman equestrian, was the first prefect. When this province was set up, the legate of Syria, P. Sulpicius Quirinus, instituted a census (which was customary for a newly created province), sparking a minor revolt against Rome led by Judas the Galilean (Acts 5:37).

The mention of Judas the Galilean provides the occasion for a digression and an important clarification, which influence the discussion of the ministry of Jesus. Until very recently, it was axiomatic to speak of a "Zealot" movement that was active throughout the first century C.E. and culminated in the revolt against Rome in 66–72 C.E.[25] Jesus' ministry, and especially his teaching on nonviolence, was often seen as counter to this movement. Paradoxically, Josephus provides the principal evidence both for and against such a view.

Josephus describes the career of Judas briefly in the *Jewish War* and in the *Jewish Antiquities* (written approximately twenty years after the *Jewish War*). The earlier account reads:

> Under his administration, a Galilaean named Judas incited his countrymen to revolt [*apostasin*], upbraiding them as cowards for

consenting to pay tribute to the Romans and for tolerating mortal masters, after having God for their Lord. This man was a sophist [translated as "sophist" in the LCL, but better, "teacher"] who founded a sect of his own, having nothing in common with the others. (*War* 2.118)

In the longer account (*Ant* 18.3-10), Josephus expands his earlier view and contradicts it on certain points, principally on the alliance between Judas and Saddok, a Pharisee. Here he explicitly describes Judas and Saddok as the founders of an alien (or intrusive) "fourth philosophy" (*Ant* 18.9). The ambiguity arises because Josephus roots the "ruin of our cause" (i.e., the ultimate destruction of Jerusalem) in the teaching of Judas and Saddok. Josephus also notes (*Ant* 20.102) that the sons of Judas, James and Simon, were crucified for sedition under Tiberius Alexander (procurator from 46–48 C.E., nephew of Philo of Alexandria). A son (or grandson) of Judas, Menahem, was a commander of the Sicarii during the siege of Jerusalem. He brutally murdered the high priest Ananias and was himself murdered by the partisans of Eleazer (son of Ananias and leader of the priestly faction during the revolt; *War* 2.433-49). Among the supporters of Menahem was his relative (a different) Eleazer, son of Jairus, who escaped from Jerusalem and later became the *despotēs* of Masada (*War* 2.447).

On the surface, it seems that Josephus describes the origin and growth of the Zealot movement in the career of Judas the Galilean, who instilled in his sons a violent revolutionary zeal. Yet, as Horsley and Hanson argue, Judas did not advocate violence (nor does Josephus say this explicitly).[26] They, along with Martin Goodman and others, argue that Zealot, used as a proper name for a violent revolutionary movement, should be reserved to those groups that were active only in the concluding years of the Jewish War (66–72).[27] They also call attention to the pro-Roman and apologetic tendencies of Josephus.[28] Somewhat like Thucydides five centuries earlier, Josephus views the source of all the evil that befell the Jews as *stasis* or *apostasis*, that is, political factionalism leading to revolt. Josephus also favors the priestly aristocracy and its policies, which tended toward accommodation to Roman rule. Josephus thus constructs a trail of rebellion originating in the early days of Rome's direct rule over Judea and culminating in the cataclysm of 70 C.E. There is, however, very little evidence that during the ministry of Jesus there was significant "revolutionary" activity or a conscious ideology of revolt against Rome. Raymond Brown states that it is necessary to distinguish carefully the political situation in Judea in the period 6–41 C.E. from that of 44–66 C.E.[29] The earlier period, which compassed the ministry of Jesus, was characterized by political stability and a lack of social unrest, as noted by the Roman historian Tacitus: under Tiberius (14–37 C.E.), "all was quiet" (*Hist* 5.9; *Ann* 12.54). Social unrest escalates after 44 C.E. when the procurators are increasingly insensitive and inept. Whatever the underlying reason for the execution of Jesus, it is no longer possible to say that he was seen as a Zealot.

I will now return to the issue of governance in Judea during the ministry of Jesus. During both the Herodian and Roman periods, the high priest, who was the virtual leader of the Jewish people, was appointed first by Herod and later by the Roman prefect or procurator.[30] (The term "prefect" should be used for Roman governors prior to Claudius [41–54 C.E.] and "procurator" after that.[31]) Between the beginning of Herod's reign in 37 B.C.E. and the coming of Herod Agrippa I in 41 C.E., there were fifteen high priests. Roman governors deposed them almost at will. What is remarkable is that one family, that of Ananus (equals Annas in the New Testament) dominated the high priesthood during this period. Ananus himself was high priest from 6–15 C.E. His son Eleazar was high priest from 16–17 C.E., and he was succeeded by Joseph Caiaphas (Yehosef bar Qafà) high priest from 18–36 C.E. (The New Testament calls him the son-in-law of Annas—a relationship affirmed by most Jewish and Christian historians.[32]) Four other sons of Annas served as high priests. Equally important for understanding the events surrounding the death of Jesus was that Pontius Pilate was prefect from 26–36 C.E. in a century when the average term for governors was between three and four years.

Because Judea was a relatively new province at a time when the Roman Empire itself was being established, its legal procedures are difficult to know with any certainty. If the pattern adopted in other provinces is a model, the Roman governor exercised his power normally through the local nobility or wealthiest classes.[33] In all likelihood, the prefect had a great deal of power, especially in capital cases and particularly in those involving non-Roman citizens and people not of the local nobility. For example, in 11 C.E., Volesus Messala, a proconsul of Asia, executed 300 people in a single day and walked about the bodies exclaiming, "*Ecce regale factum.*"[34] Despite sporadic outbreaks of violence brought on by the insensitive behavior of Pilate, the province of Judea was generally stable and peaceful during the time in office of Caiaphas and Pilate. Cooperation rather than confrontation must have characterized their relationship.[35]

Events Surrounding the Death of Jesus

My principal aim in this admittedly inadequate survey of aspects of the history and governance of Judea during the initial decades of the Common Era has been to prepare for a somewhat hypothetical reconstruction of the events surrounding the execution of Jesus.

It is important to recall that civil unrest and messianic movements characterized the last years of the Herodians. I suggest that these events remained vivid in the memory of the high priest Annas and his family. During his tenure and that of his family, the province remained relatively peaceful. Sanders, in his recent, important study of the Jewish practice and belief from 63 B.C.E. to 66 C.E., calls attention to the ambiguous state of the Jerusalem chief priests (that is, high priests, former high priests, and members of the priestly nobility). Often, they are criticized for their wealth and oppressive practices. Sanders notes that "some were corrupt, out for their own gain and that of their sycophants, while some used their power and influence to protect the people from direct intervention from Rome. . . . To complicate our assessment even further, one person could fall into both camps."[36] Josephus narrates that the servants of the chief priests collected tithes from the threshing floor, with the result that some of the ordinary priests starved (*Ant* 20.180-81). The ornate ossuaries in the recently discovered burial chamber of Caiaphas and his family suggest a high degree of wealth. A coin found in the mouth of one of the adult women suggests the assimilation of the pagan custom of payment to the god Charon for safe passage over the river Styx.[37] This might also suggest that Caiaphas, in addition to being relatively wealthy, had made major accommodations to Hellenism. Yet, Sanders concludes his survey of the different leadership groups:

> The various actors in the period that we have surveyed are often the objects of moral censure. We shall understand them better if we view them sympathetically. I rather like the chief priests. I think that on the whole they tried hard and did better at staving off revolt and protecting the Jewish population from Roman troops than any other group could have done—except a succession of Herods.[38]

The most difficult question surrounding the death of Jesus is that he was crucified, as Nils Dahl (followed by Donald Juel) has continually stressed, *as a Messiah.*[39] The *titulus* on the cross, found substantially the same in all the Gospels, is "king of the Jews"—a title with messianic overtones (even if placed there as mockery by Pilate).[40] The mode of execution, public crucifixion, was used by the Romans normally for people thought to be serious threats to the public order, especially those seen to be threats to Roman sovereignty.[41] With the demise of the "revolutionary Jesus" hypothesis (see above), the problem is even more acute: Why would Jesus be "the crucified Messiah"? The problem is also complicated by the fact that there is a growing consensus that Jesus in his lifetime did not claim to be the Messiah. Raymond Brown conducts a careful review of the question, "Was Jesus called the Messiah before his resurrection?" and underlines two facts agreed on by virtually all contemporary scholars: (1) "after the resurrection Jesus was called the Messiah (Jesus Christ, Jesus the Christ, Christ of God) with astounding frequency," and (2) "scenes in the Gospel in which Jesus is addressed or acknowledged as the Messiah are very few and acceptance of that title by Jesus is marred by complication."[42] Brown then expands on these facts and concludes that it is "plausible that during Jesus' lifetime some of his followers thought him to be the Messiah, that is, the expected anointed king of the House of David who would rule over God's people" and that "Jesus, confronted with this identification responded ambivalently."[43] We are faced then with a problem posed acutely by William Wrede at the beginning of this century—how a basically unmessianic life of Jesus could give rise to the proclamation of him as *christos* or Messiah.[44]

At the risk of philological overload, another terminological clarification is necessary. "Messiah" has both a narrow usage and extended usage. The former is principally for a *royal* figure; the latter is extended to a variety of saving figures. Two contemporary authors underscore the differences. Joseph Fitzmyer (an advocate of the narrow meaning) writes:

> In the time of the Jesus the title "Messiah" would have denoted an expected anointed agent sent by God either in the Davidic, kingly or political tradition for the restoration of Israel and the triumph of God's power and dominion or in the priestly tradition (see 2 *Esdr* 12:32; 1 *Enoch* 48:10; 52:4; *Pss. Sol.* 17:32; 18:5, 7; 1QS 9:11).[45]

Zwi Werblowsky describes the extended usage as follows:

103

It is hardly necessary to remind ourselves that the word "Messiah," derived from the Hebrew *mashah* (anoint) denotes a person with a special mission from God . . . . Hence in a broader and metaphorical sense, the term "Messiah" can signify any man or office bearer charged with a special task or function.[46]

Werblowsky then notes that the term was applied to the eschatological Davidic Messiah and further comments:

Hence messianism has been, and is, used in a broad and at times very loose sense to refer to beliefs and theories regarding an eschatological or at the least very radical improvement of the state of man, society and the world (or cosmos as a whole) or even a final consummation of history.[47]

The issue is further complicated by significant questions raised about Jewish Messianism in the major volume emanating from a conference held at Princeton in 1987, and subsequently published.[48] The studies, by leading scholars in each area, cover the Hebrew Bible, the literature of early Judaism, and emergent Christianity and have significant implications for the manner in which theologians deal with New Testament Christology.

After noting earlier that "[the] term 'the Messiah' simply does not appear in the Hebrew Scriptures or the Old Testament,"[49] James H. Charlesworth summarizes the major conclusions of the conference in five propositions (slightly abbreviated here):

1. Jewish messianology exploded into the history of ideas in the early first century B.C.E., and not earlier, because of the degeneration of the Hasmonean dynasty, because of their royal claims, and then because of the loss of the land to gentile (i.e., Roman) rulers.

2. Jews did not profess a coherent and normative messianology.

3. New Testament scholars must read and attempt to master all the early Jewish writings.

4. One can no longer claim that most Jews were looking for the coming of the Messiah.

5. The Gospels and Paul must not be read as if they are reliable sources for pre-70 C.E. Jewish messianic beliefs.[50]

I doubt that all of Charlesworth's conclusions would be accepted by scholars working on early Judaism and the New Testament (and perhaps not by all the participants in the conference), but they are a caution against an overly facile understanding of Jesus as Messiah.

Any attempt to address the problems surrounding the execution of Jesus must account for two factors: (1) why Jesus was thought to be such a threat to Roman power that he suffered crucifixion, rather than some lesser penalty, and (2) why he is crucified *as Messiah*.[51] I stress the hypothetical nature of my proposal, which is put forth to evoke discussion rather than to offer conclusive solutions. My proposal is that Caiaphas, select other members of the priestly aristocracy, and Pontius Pilate had grounds for viewing Jesus as a threat to the public order, which they then interpreted in "messianic" terms, even if Jesus never claimed such a messiahship. I will center on three bits of evidence that may support such a hypothesis.

The Relationship of Jesus and John the Baptizer. The first evidence is the relationship of Jesus and John the Baptizer. In a recent and important article, which is part of a projected full-scale study of Jesus, Jerome Murphy-O'Connor suggests that, in the initial stages of his ministry, Jesus was a disciple of John the Baptist.[52] The argument unfolds as follows. John 1:35-42, although clearly subordinating John the Baptizer to Jesus, suggests that Jesus' first disciples had formerly been disciples of John and had joined Jesus after his baptism by and separation from John (see Acts 2:21-22). John 3:26 and 4:1 may indicate that the initial ministry of Jesus was *in Judea* and similar to that of John. This is confirmed by the Synoptic data

105

where Jesus begins his ministry in *Galilee* only after the arrest of John. Murphy-O'Connor argues then that Jesus began his public career as a disciple of John and later went in a different direction.

Another important element in this relationship is the preaching of John. John did not preach the coming of God's reign, but imminent and apocalyptic judgment. Also, on the basis of both Q (Matt 3:1-11; Luke 3:2-9) and Mark 1:4-5, John had success among the people in preaching a baptism of repentance for the forgiveness of sin. This was coupled with a strong message of judgment against the powerful (Matt 3:7-10; Luke 3:7-9), which, in the Judean context, could be the opulent life-style of the Jerusalem nobility or the priestly aristocracy, criticized also in Jewish sources (Josephus *Ant.* 20.180-81). John was subsequently executed by Herod Antipas. In the gospels, it is because he castigated Herod for his adulterous marriage, but Josephus says that Antipas feared John was leading a mass movement (*stasis*) that was politically dangerous (*Ant.* 18.118-19).[53] Therefore, early in what might have been a relatively short career, Jesus would have been associated with the radical preaching of John. Because the bulk of Jesus' teaching took place in Galilee (according to the Synoptics), it is possible that Jerusalem officials, both Roman and Jewish, would have known Jesus principally as a disciple of John and perhaps even as the one to whom John pointed as "stronger than I" (Matt 3:11; Mark 1:7; Luke 3:16). There is also evidence that, at times, the work of Jesus and that of John were confused. On two occasions, the Gospel of Mark records the opinion of both the crowd and Herod Antipas: that Jesus is "John the Baptizer, raised from the dead" (6:14) or simply "John the Baptist" (8:28). Because the tendency in the developing gospel tradition is clearly to distinguish John and to subordinate John to Jesus, this early confusion has a high claim to be an authentic recollection of popular opinion at the time of Jesus.[54] Both Jewish and Roman officials in Jerusalem might well have seen Jesus as the same kind of threat as the recently executed John.

106

Jesus' Action in the Temple. The second point of evidence is the difficult issue surrounding Jesus' action in the temple, recounted in all four Gospels (Matt 21:12-13; Mark 11:15-19; Luke 19:45-48; John 2:13-22). Although John places this act early in the ministry of Jesus and the Synoptics have it near the end of his life, it is unanimously in a context of Passover. There are minor variations, but the substance of the narrative is the same. In all accounts, Jesus is in the temple area, drives out sellers and buyers (Luke omits buyers), and overturns the tables of the money changers. In the Synoptics, Jesus justifies this by a reminder that the house will be a house of prayer for all nations (Isa 56:7) but also cites the temple sermon of Jeremiah 7, that "you" have turned it into a den of robbers. In John, the scriptural quote is Psalm 69:9, "Zeal for your house will consume me."

The principal reason that I use the ambiguous term "Jesus' action in the temple," rather than the traditional designation "cleansing of the temple," is that how to name the incident is precisely what is disputed. Sanders is one of those who argue strongly that the action is not a cleansing or purification, but a symbolic act signifying the impending destruction of the temple.[55] For Sanders, such an action is part of Jesus' "restorationist eschatology," where Jesus points to a new and glorious temple that will be built by God. Paula Fredriksen strongly seconds Sanders' view:

> But in the context of his ministry, and more broadly in the context of Jewish restoration theology, such destruction is not "negative"; it necessarily implies no condemnation of e.g. the Temple cult, the Torah, Judaism, or anything else. In the idiom of Jewish apocalyptic, destruction implies rebuilding; and a new or renewed temple—especially one not made by the hand of man [Mark 14:58]—would imply, more directly, that the Kingdom of God was at hand.[56]

Although I find elements of this position agreeable, I find more persuasive a recent study by Craig Evans,[57] who argues for the

107

more traditional interpretation that Jesus' action is a "cleansing" in the sense of being a protest against the commercialism of the temple. Evans's arguments are numerous; I will mention some of the important ones:

1. In other places in the Gospels, the Evangelists do not hesitate to have Jesus predict the destruction of the temple (e.g., Mark 13:1-2 and parallels).

2. The Markan insertion of the cleansing of the temple between the beginning and end of the cursing of the barren fig tree suggests that the real problem with the temple is that it is not bearing "fruit."

3. Although there are pre-Christian texts that portray the Messiah as temple builder, there is none that suggests a messianic figure will herald the destruction of the temple and then rebuild it.

4. In a large number of biblical texts and postbiblical texts, prophetic figures criticize corruption in the use of temple resources.

5. There is some evidence, Evans claims, for greed and corruption among certain high priestly families of the time of Jesus. Evans calls attention to a 1964 article by V. Eppstein, who argued from rabbinic texts that the business of selling sacrificial objects was brought into the temple under the administration of the family of Annas.[58]

To these I would add that the logic of Sanders' restorationist eschatology is not that the temple be destroyed as a prelude to a new temple, but that it be "restored" to its earlier integrity.

I am ready to accept Evans's defense of the more traditional interpretation of Jesus' action, but I am not satisfied with the word "cleansing." No term like this is used in the accounts themselves and it suggests that in some way the temple worship was "impure" or "unclean." I would prefer to call the incident (somewhat cumbersomely), "Jesus' prophetic protest against mercantile activity in the temple." Given the size of the temple precincts as well as the vast crowds gathered for the Passover feast, Jesus' action may have been a symbolic protest against a number of buyers and sellers rather than a wholesale expulsion of them, as the Gospels suggest. Because the temple was at the center of the religious and economic life of Jerusalem, any disturbance in it, especially associated with crowds at Passover, would cause serious concern among the high priests, the priestly aristocracy, and temple officials.

The Handing Over and Arrest of Jesus. The third bit of evidence I call attention to is the handing over and arrest of Jesus. Firmly fixed in the tradition is that Jesus was "handed over" by Judas, called "one of the twelve," that is, one of those summoned by Jesus to be the nucleus of the eschatological Israel (Matt 19:28).[59] This incident has a high claim to authenticity: it is scarcely the kind of thing that would have been made up by the early church. The "Judas tradition," however, shows signs of development, from the simple mention of Judas as the one who handed over Jesus (Mark 3:19) to a stress on the malice of the chief priests (Mark 14:10-11) and on Judas's betrayal as a fulfillment of scripture (John 13:18).[60] My principal concern is with the arrest of Jesus where, in all the Gospels, Judas plays a leading role. In John 18:3, Judas as leader of the arresting band "procures" a squad of Roman soldiers and temple police. Most intriguing in this pericope is the virtual identical saying attributed to Jesus in the Synoptic Gospels (Matt 26:55; Mark 14:48; Luke 22:53): "Have you come out as against a bandit (*Lēstēn*) with swords and clubs to capture me. Day after day I was in the temple teaching and you did not seize me." The word *lēstēs* has the overtones of social banditry, that is, bandits who were threats to the public order. Mark (15:7), for example, notes that Barabbas was a "bandit" who had committed murder during an insurrection (*meta tōn stasiastōn*, also

109

possibly translated "with those involved in an insurrection"). One of the most intriguing aspects of Mark 14:48 and parallels is why Jesus should have been arrested by an armed guard prepared for violent resistance and subsequently crucified as a *lēstēs* (Mark 15:27), when there is no direct evidence in the Gospels that he advocated or was involved in violence.

My suggestion is that the "betrayal" of Judas is precisely that *he misrepresented Jesus* as a public threat to the Romans and to the temple authorities. This is the only way, I feel, to explain the tradition of the armed arrest. This may also explain the fact that, in John's Gospel, Jesus is not tried formally before a Jewish court, but simply is questioned by the high priest (most likely, Annas) "about his disciples and about his teaching" (John 18:19). It is feasible that the high priest was seeking more accurate information from Jesus himself. At this point, and perhaps forever, we possess inadequate information on what might have motivated Judas to misrepresent the Jesus movement, nor do we have enough evidence to know whether Jesus ever explained his teaching to his accusers. In John 18:20, Jesus denies any secret teaching and tells the high priest to question those who heard his teaching. Given the heavy theological and dramatic overlay in the Johannine passion narrative, it is doubtful that this represents a recorded response of Jesus.

Further comments on the role of Annas (and his family who followed him in the high priesthood) in the execution of Jesus may be helpful. If, as I said earlier, Annas, who according to John still exercised much power, had vivid memories of the chaos caused two decades earlier by messianic pretenders, he would naturally have been concerned about a resurgence of such movements. Jesus' association with John, his popular teaching (recall that Judas the Galilean was a *sophistēs*), and his attacks against the aristocratic classes (Matt 11:8; Mark 10:42; Luke 7:24) might have evoked clear memories of Judas and of the earlier civil disturbances that followed the death of Herod the Great. In this vein, Ferus Millar has suggested that John's Gospel may contain historical traditions that are closer to actual events than are those in the Synoptics.[61] The Johannine Jesus, for example, appears at least twice in Jerusalem before his final visit and precipitates opposition among Jerusalem officials (John 7:32; cf. Mark 3:22). In John, prior to Jesus' last week in Jerusalem, Caiaphas and the chief priests plan to arrest him (John 11:45-53), but the actual examination of Jesus is conducted by Annas (John 18:12-24). The theory that Caiaphas and Pilate must have had a strong working relationship geared to the maintenance of public order is supported by the action of the Roman legate, Vitellius, in deposing Caiaphas shortly after the recall of Pilate in 36 C.E.[62] A final bit of evidence on the antagonism of the house of Annas toward the Jesus movement is Josephus' account of the death of James, the brother of Jesus (*Ant.* 20.197-203). Josephus locates the execution between the death of the procurator, Portius Festus (C.E. 62), and the arrival of Lucceius Albinus (C.E. 62–64). The high priest at this time was "Ananus" (Annas), the fifth and youngest son of the elder Annas.[63] Josephus writes of him: "He followed the school of the Sadducees, who are indeed more heartless than any of the other Jews, as I have already explained, when they sit in judgment" (*Ant.* 20.199). Josephus then narrates that Annas convened a court, which quickly judged James and ordered him to be stoned, a decision that offended "those who were strict in the observance of the law" (*Ant.* 20.201). When this group complained of Annas's action to Herod Agrippa and to Albinus, Agrippa deposed Annas from office.

To summarize briefly, my thesis is that Jesus' earlier association with John, his action in the temple, and a possible misrepresentation of his position by Judas might have been issues that caused Caiaphas and certain of his advisers (especially his father-in-law, Annas) to consult with Pilate about "the Jesus problem." The literary critical problems with both the Sanhedrin trial and the trial before Pilate suggest that Jesus might have appeared in an informal hearing before both groups. Pilate, who bears the prime responsibility for the crucifixion, had the legal power to condemn someone like Jesus, a non-Roman of no standing but under significant suspicion, with virtually no reason and perhaps with little compunction.[64] The seemingly mocking title of Jesus as "king of the Jews" could have arisen from Pilate's perception that Jesus was de facto a messianic pretender, even though Pilate had little solid evidence for this. Pilate is later recalled for incompetence, but there is no record that he was ever rebuked for the crucifixion of Jesus. In fact, the Roman historian Tacitus, who castigates Pilate's patron Sejanus, speaks with implicit approval of Pilate's execution of Jesus (*Ann.* 15.44).

Connections between the Death of Jesus and His Life

Thus far I have attempted to suggest some reasons why Jesus would have been seen as a serious threat to political stability and why the Roman governor and temple aristocracy would have grounds for collusion in his execution. Still unresolved is the relation between the *titulus*, "the king of the Jews," and the earthly life of Jesus. As mentioned, Nils Dahl has argued most strongly that the only explanation for the early and wide diffusion of *Christos* (Messiah) as a title and virtual proper name for Jesus is that he was the "crucified Messiah." Unfortunately, limitations of space preclude a full engagement with this issue and with other equally important issues, such as the charge of blasphemy and how Jesus articulated his relation to God.

One area of current fruitful investigation is the linkage between the kingdom proclamation of Jesus and his execution. Although it is true that in all likelihood Jesus was not addressed as a royal Messiah during his lifetime and resisted royal acclamation, he spoke constantly of the "kingdom of God."[65] Jesus' mighty works are symbols of the imminence of the kingdom, "if by the finger [in Matthew, "spirit"] of God, I cast out demons, then the kingdom of God has come upon you" (Q: Matt 12:28; Luke 11:20). Other wonder workers are attested in first-century Jewish sources, but none conjoins these mighty deeds with the advent of the kingdom. Dennis Duling has shown that, in many intertestamental texts, exorcisms and healing are associated with Solomon (obviously a royal figure and a son of David), a connection made explicit in the New Testament.[66] Many of the kingdom sayings that have a high claim to authenticity also suggest conflict or clash of kingdoms (Q: Matt 12:22-30; Luke 11:14-23; see also Mark 3:20-27). The reversal expected in God's kingdom can be construed as a threat to people of power and influence (Matt 5:3; Mark 10:23-25; Luke 6:20, *et par*; Mark 10:35-42, *et par*). The entry of Jesus into Jerusalem, as Evans shows, is described in language evocative of royal motifs.[67] In most New Testament traditions, Jesus is of Davidic origin. John Meier makes the interesting observation that the "patriarchal" names of his brothers (James, Joses, Jude, and Simon [Mark 6:3]), as well as his putative father's name "Joseph," suggest that "Jesus' family may have shared in the reawakening of Jewish national and religious identity which looked forward to the restoration of Israel in its fully glory. This is all the more likely if Joseph claimed to be a descendant of King David."[68]

I would also add here that, although wide agreement is emerging about recent research that cautions against a too free use of the term "messianic" or its application to first-century figures who cause social unrest, there is a chance that contemporary scholars are making subtle distinctions that were not always made in the first century. It is illegitimate to call everyone from Ezekias, the bandit chieftain of 47 B.C.E. (Josephus, *War* 1.204-7; *Ant.* 14.159-60), to Simon bar Giora a "messianic pretender," but there were certain significant figures who claimed royal prerogatives. John Dominic Crossan lists five cases of "Messiahs" between 4 B.C.E. and 68–70 C.E., all of whom claimed royal power, even if they are not called "the" or "a" Messiah. They are: (1) in Galilee, 4 B.C.E., Judas, son of the bandit leader Ezekias (*War* 2.56; *Ant.* 17.271-72); (2) in Perea,

4 B.C.E., Simon the Herodian slave (*War* 2.57-59; *Ant.* 17.273-77); (3) in Judea, 4 B.C.E., Athronges, the shepherd (*War* 2.60-65; *Ant.* 17.278-84); (4) Menahem, (grand)son of Judas the Galilean (*War* 2.433-434, 444); (5) Simon, son of Gioras (bar Giora) (*War* 2.521, 652-54; 4.503-10, 529; 7.26-36, 154).[69] The significance of this list as a contribution to understanding attitudes toward Jesus is in the high proportion of Galileans involved in these messianic uprisings, and in the rise of explicit messianic claims during periods of turmoil (after the death of Herod and in the final stages of the Jewish war). As Crossan suggests, Tacitus' phrase *sub Tiberio quies*, often invoked to claim that there were no messianic movements during the ministry of Jesus, may simply mean that they were suppressed or had gone underground. As an example, Ezekias, the Galilean bandit chief, had a son and a grandson who claimed messianic credentials and who surfaced in Josephus' narrative at times of explicit social upheaval. Judea may have been quiet, but messianic movements may have been percolating during the period of Jesus' ministry.

Summary of the Trial and Death of Jesus

A minimalist view of the historical events would suggest the collusion of some Jewish temple authorities with Pilate in the crucifixion of Jesus. The degree of initiative and the extent of the collusion are very difficult to determine. Jewish implication in the death of Jesus is attested in a statement found in the Babylonian Talmud, tractate *Sanhedrin* 43a, although its independent value is highly debated. It contains a reference to a Yeshu (Jesus) who was hanged on the eve of the Passover because he practiced magic and led Israel astray.[70] To speak of some Jewish involvement is, however, a far cry from the malice attributed to Jews as a group in the New Testament itself and in subsequent church history. Raymond Brown gives important guidelines to Christians for assessing Jewish involvement in the death of Jesus.[71] First, one must understand that religious

114

people could have disliked Jesus. Brown notes that "more than likely were Jesus to appear in our time (with the challenge re-phrased in terms of contemporary religious stances) and be arrested and tried again, most of those finding him guilty would identify themselves as Christians and think they were rejecting an im-poster."[72] Second, in Jesus' time, religious opposition often led to violence. Brown calls attention to an unnamed high priest in the second century B.C.E. who sought the death of the Essene Teacher of Righteousness (1QpHab 11:2-8), and to disputes between the Pharisees and the Sadducees during the Hasmonean period.[73] Third, he distinguishes between "responsibility" and guilt. It is one thing to say that certain Jews in the first century bore some respon-sibility for the death of Jesus and to attribute guilt to a whole peo-ple. Finally, Brown compares the careers of Jesus and Jeremiah. Jeremiah was "a disturbing challenger of the religious structures of his time" and warned about the imminent destruction of the temple (Jer 7:1-15). Priests and (false) prophets tried to persuade the peo-ple that Jeremiah deserved death (26:1-15) and the nobles tried to persuade the king to execute him (38:1-5).[74] The cases of Jesus and Jeremiah were inner Jewish disputes, and, for both Jews and Chris-tians, Jeremiah is an example of a righteous person persecuted by religious leaders. In the case of Jesus, however, a great difference arises because "those who thought that Jesus was right became an-other religion. Jews and Christians were not able to say in this in-stance that one of *our own* whom God raised up was made to suffer by *our* leaders."[75] The actions of first-century Jewish leaders, in try-ing to maintain a balance between a volatile populace, made even more so by the Passover festival, and a brutal Roman power, should not be judged too harshly from our perspective. Christian religious leaders throughout the centuries have often chosen detente with oppressive political power rather than advocacy of a "disturbing challenger of the religious structures," especially when resistance would have led to greater suffering.

FROM CRUCIFIED MESSIAH TO RISEN CHRIST

Given the limitation of space, I cannot elaborate adequately on the second major thrust of my essay: how Jesus crucified as Messiah became the risen Christ of the early kerygma. Again, I call attention to the work of Nils Dahl and Donald Juel, especially Juel's recent work, *Messianic Exegesis: Christological Interpretation of the Old Testament in Early Christianity*. These authors, among others, call attention to the extraordinarily rapid and diverse Christological development in the years following the death of Jesus. By the time of the pre-Pauline formula in 1 Corinthians 15:3-8, which may date back to the early 40s of the first century, *Christos* is already virtually a proper name rather than a description: "For I hand on to you as of first importance what I in turn had received that Christ died for our sins in accordance with the scriptures, and that he was buried and that he was raised on the third day" (see also Rom 1:3-4). The still unsolved question of Christology is how *christos* (the Greek translation for Messiah) lost many of the royal connotations it possessed in Jewish literature and became so quickly a virtual proper name for the risen Jesus. I can only mention here a few directions that I would hope subsequently to explore more fully.

Any explorations must now take into account the immense amount of work simply on messianic expectation in earliest Judaism, contained in the excellent studies by leading scholars in *The Messiah: Developments in Earliest Judaism and Christianity*, which I mentioned above. In summarizing the research, Charlesworth notes "that messianology does not easily flow into Christology," for "no other title would have been so difficult to align with the life and thought of Jesus."[76]

The result of the research gathered here and supported by other scholars is that we cannot solve the problem of how the early Christians came to call the risen Jesus "Messiah," or "Lord," or any other title, simply by finding a precedent in early Judaism, a sort of mold into which Jesus can be poured. As Juel has so well shown, Christology, or early Christian understanding of Jesus, is due to the creative exegetical activity of early Christians wrestling with significant texts of their Jewish heritage such as Nathan's oracle in 2 Samuel 7:10-17.[77] Juel shows how this text, which was important to both the people at Qumran and to early Christians, as well as other texts (e.g., Pss 22, 31, 69, and especially 89), provide the material out of which early Christians proclaimed the risen Messiah.[78]

However much the early Christians drew on exegetical traditions, it is the proclamation of the resurrection that provides the generating force for the development. What lies behind this proclamation is in the realm of faith, not historical research. Paula Fredriksen states the issue well: "We can draw securely from this evidence [i.e., the resurrection proclamation] only the baldest conclusion: that despite the absolute certainty of Jesus' death, his immediate followers with equal certainty perceived—and then proclaimed that Jesus lived again."[79] Fredriksen further argues that their resurrection faith made the early Christians affirm that the resurrection of Jesus was his vindication and a sign that the kingdom he failed to usher in before his death was now imminent.[80] I would add to these comments the observation that the terms used for resurrection in the New Testament, especially the verbs *egeirein* and *anistēmi*, do not, as in modern consciousness, suggest primarily return to life, but, following the Septuagint, have the overtone of "installation to a function, rising to an action, sending a historical figure or inaugurating a course of affairs."[81] In the "messianic oracle" of 2 Samuel 7:12, the Lord says that he will "raise up" (*anastēsō*) a descendant of David.

This language of raising up/royal installation, as Barnabas Lindars has cogently argued, is in debt also to the early Christian use of Psalm 16:8-11 and Psalm 110:1.[82] The combination of deliverance from death and placing "at the right hand" of the Lord in Psalm 16:10-11, and the placing of the Davidic king at the right hand of the Lord in Psalm 110:1 enabled early Christians to interpret the resurrection of Jesus as his deliverance from death and his royal installation (Acts 2:33; see Rom 8:34; Eph 1:20; Col 3:1; Heb 1:3, 13; 8:1; 10:12; 12:2; 1 Pet 3:22). The raising up of Jesus, whatever it was objectively or in the experience of the early believers, was interpreted as the royal installation of the crucified Messiah as the risen Christ.

The work of Juel and Lindars has implications for another aspect of contemporary historical Jesus research, as well as for the origin of Christology. Certain tendencies are countered by the research of Juel and Lindars, especially the interpretation of the Jesus movement as a gathering of itinerant, charismatic "peasants."[83] Burton Mack, among others, proposes a "cynic Jesus" heavily influenced by Hellenistic ethos and thought forms. This runs the risk of "de-Judaizing" Jesus.[84] Shortly after the resurrection, Jesus' first followers turn to the Hebrew Scriptures and use them in a sophisticated and nuanced way to construct both an apology for the death of Jesus and a theological interpretation of its significance. Josephus states that the Jews pride themselves in the education of their children (Ag. Ap. 1.60; see 2.171-72) and says that literacy is a national legacy: "[T]he Law orders that they [children] be taught to read, and shall learn both the laws and the deeds of their ancestors [progonōn]" (Ag. Ap. 2.204). This would support the position that Jesus and his first followers were not simple "peasants" but were conversant in the Hebrew Scriptures and in diverse methods of interpretation.

A FINAL WORD

This essay originated as part of a dialogue between Jewish and Christian scholars over issues of concern to both communities. My principal aim has been to address certain historical issues surrounding the trial of Jesus and to hint at theological developments of Jesus as Messiah in early Christianity. I want to end on a more personal note. The first followers of Jesus believed that Jesus would soon restore the kingdom to Israel (Acts 1:6); virtually all of the first generation of Christians expected Jesus to return soon as the glorious Messiah who would establish his kingdom (Mark 9:1; 13:24-26, *et par*; Rom 13:11-14; 1 Cor 15:20-28; 16:22; 1 Thess 4:13-18). Both the original followers of Jesus and the first generation of Christians were disappointed, and Christians today still await the fulfillment of the messianic age promised by the Hebrew Scriptures and the New Testament. Hope for a coming Messiah is part of traditional Jewish theology. For Christians, the Messiah has not returned; for Jews he is still awaited. Rabbi Herschel Matt described well the shared hopes of Jews and Christians.

> Jews and Christians—our situations are somewhat different; our roles and tasks are somewhat different; our styles and modes are somewhat different. But we are covenanted to and by the same God of Israel; our essential teachings are markedly similar; our goals, identical. And the one whose second coming Christians await and whose (first) coming we Jews await—when he comes—will surely turn out to have the same face for all of us.[85]

As Christians and Jews, although our hopes remain unfulfilled, we share a radical longing for the vision of the new age heralded by Isaiah:

> On this mountain the Lord of Hosts will make for all peoples a feast of rich food, a feast of well-aged wines, of rich food filled with marrow of well-aged wines strained clear, and he will destroy on this mountain the shroud that is cast over all peoples, the sheet that is spread over all nations; he will swallow up death for ever (Isa 25:6-7)

and

> On that day the deaf shall hear the words of a scroll, and out of their gloom and darkness the eyes of the blind shall see. The meek shall obtain fresh joy in the Lord, and the neediest people shall exult in the Holy One of Israel (Isa 29:18-19).

Despite the horrible history of Christian persecution of Jews, for which I, as a Christian, am constantly ashamed, and in the face of continued misunderstanding between Christians and Jews, it is my constant hope that we can anticipate in our lives and strive to implement together in our society that same peace and justice that Torah and Testament have so eloquently promised.

For Discussion

1. Are the trial narratives in the Gospels a record of what historically actually happened to Jesus or are they theological interpretations? If interpretations, what is the significance for Jewish–Christian relations?

2. From reading this chapter, what is your new understanding of the Sanhedrin?

3. Summarize the governance in Judea during the ministry of Jesus. How is one to understand the term "Zealot" during this period?

4. What is the most difficult question surrounding the death of Jesus and what are its implications for Jewish–Christian dialogue?

5. What are the two usages of the term "Messiah" and what are the implications for interpreting New Testament texts? Is there a danger of an overly facile understanding of Jesus as Messiah?

6. What are two factors that must be accounted for when addressing problems surrounding the execution of Jesus?

7. How does the author suggest one wrestle with Jesus' action in the temple and why is the author of the chapter so reluctant to call it a "cleansing"?

8. How does one relate the title on the cross, "the king of the Jews," and the earthly life of Jesus? What are the complexities involved and how do these relate to Jewish–Christian dialogue?

9. What important guidelines should be followed by Christians in assessing Jewish involvement in the death of Jesus? Explain.

10. From reading this chapter, what new insights or understandings do you have about the complexities surrounding the trial of Jesus, the use of the title "Messiah," and the risen Christ?

PART FOUR

FROM CHRIST TO GOD

7

OUTLINING THE QUESTION: FROM CHRIST TO GOD

ALAN F. SEGAL

◼

INTRODUCTION

The basic problem in Christian–Jewish relations can be understood from the conversation I heard between my grandfather and his next-door neighbor, Mr. Connolly. My grandfather was very proud of his being one of the first Jews to move from the east side of Worcester, Massachusetts, to the west side, where he was no longer living in a ghetto. When they finally let down their hair, Grandpa Segal finally blurted out,

"I don't know how you can believe in the New Testament, with all the miracles."

Then Connolly replied, "But what about the Old Testament, with the crossing of the Red Sea, the whale swallowing Jonah, fire from heaven igniting Elijah's sacrifice on Carmel, and all the many other miracles."

"Vott miracles?" my grandfather replied. "Those are the facts."

The problem in studying Christian–Jewish relations is that one community's miracles are the other community's facts. This will turn out to be a problem every time we look at one community in detail.

My task is to outline the question of from Christ to God. And since I will want to talk about the converse, I should call it: From Christ to God and back to Christ for the double play.

Baseball aside, it is a double play. In order to understand how Christianity arose from Judaism we have to understand both the similarities between Judaism and Christianity and the differences between them. The best way to do this is to look at the two terms that we have: Messiah/Christ on the one hand and Lord/Kyrios on the other. In doing so, we will illustrate both the similarities and the differences between Judaism and Christianity on these key issues. These differences and similarities can be seen most clearly by analyzing both the Jewish scriptural traditions and the specific events that founded the Christian community. Jewish tradition gives us the context for Christianity, but no prior Jewish traditions actually predict the rise of Christianity. There is no single prophecy that one can say was unambiguously fulfilled by Christianity. As I have learned from Donald Juel, in his very important book, *Messianic Exegesis,*[1] and from Nils Dahl,[2] who has now returned to his native Oslo after a full career in the United States: what does explain Christian notions of the Messiah and God are Jewish notions of the importance of interpreting scripture together with the unique events surrounding Jesus' last days.

The Messiah

On the face of it, Judaism and Christianity share single concepts of a messiah. From the New Testament's perspective, the concept of a messiah is the single most consistent concept linking the Hebrew Bible with the Christian church. The Jews expected a messiah. Jesus came. Those who accepted him became Christians. The rest of the Jews denied him.

Would that history were as simple as that. The concept of a messiah, as it appears in Christianity, scarcely appears in the Hebrew Bible at all and only vaguely appears in the other sectarian literature of the day. Messiah, of course, is an anglicized form of the Hebrew word *mashiah*, which means "anointed one." Anointing was one way that Hebrew society could install its officers. At our inaugurations, we ask our officers to swear on the Bible to protect and defend the Constitution of the United States. In European monarchies, like Greco-Roman societies, kings and victors are crowned. Therefore, the word "messiah" means the currently anointed ruler, and that is how it is used throughout the Hebrew Bible. No Greek knew what a messiah was because the Greeks did not anoint kings. The only association was with athletics: wrestlers especially oiled their bodies before competing. So, to a Greek, messiah just sounded like "Mr. Shampooed Man."

Thus, we cannot from the historical evidence assume that Judean society had a fixed concept of messiah at all. There was no job description, for which Jesus applied and received the job. Nobody advertised it in the *Village Voice:* "WANTED: ONE SINGLE JEWISH MALE MESSIAH 170 lbs 6' looking for the coming kingdom or foxy lady, whatever comes first." If this were so, there would not have been a Jewish–Christian controversy. Judaism was the only people in the whole world who knew what a messiah was. In fact, Judaism had many different and conflicting ideas of the messiah, but none that fit the Christian case. Indeed, anyone who knows anything at all about the New Testament in a critical, scholarly way knows that *messiah* is the single most problematic term in the church's vocabulary of titles for Jesus. Jesus does not seem himself to have wanted such a title and there is relatively little evidence that he ever applied the term to himself.

127

The Hebrew Bible can use the word messiah to refer to many things. Saul's shield is described as anointed. The people are anointed. Even Cyrus the Persian is described as *the* messiah (Is 45:1). When the Hebrew Bible uses the word messiah to describe the king of Judah, it always means the reigning king.

The Hebrew Bible does occasionally (especially in the later books) have a sense that there will be a future ideal ruler. But, strangely enough, it does not designate this ideal ruler with the term messiah. The terms are "branch" or son of David. In other words, there is no future messiah in the Hebrew Bible at all. Nor is there one in the Mishnah. Nor is there in the Apocrypha.

There is, in a very few documents, a concept of an expected, future messiah. They are the Old Testament Pseudepigrapha. You may not have even heard of them. They are so obscure that no one read them for centuries. Until the discovery of the Dead Sea Scrolls and the publication of *Old Testament Pseudepigrapha,* edited by James H. Charlesworth, they were scarcely known outside of scholarly circles.[3]

Furthermore, the Dead Sea Scrolls, which contain many pseudepigraphical writings, don't really have much of a concept of the messiah either. He's there but he's not given a big part. In fact, there are at least two different messiahs at Qumran, the place where the Dead Sea Scrolls were found. The messiah whom they particularly like is the anointed of Aaron, not the anointed of David. In other words, being priests, they look to a descendant of the priestly line, a messiah of Aaron. This seems to demonstrate the fluidity of the concept.[4]

Even when there is a doctrine of the end of time, there doesn't need to be a messiah. The messiah was not a necessary part of the drama. Lots of discussions of the coming end of time do not speak of a messiah at all. Some even speak of other figures, like the Son of man. Nor is the messiah viewed as weak or suffering, before Christianity. Indeed, the whole idea of the messiah, before Christianity, was that he was going to give the Romans a pasting. Everybody could fail. Everyone else might suffer. But the point of the messiah, as opposed to prophets and servants of the Lord, was that the messiah, being the rightful king of Israel, was going to kick someone's butt.

The whole idea of a messiah is rare in Judaism but what's even more shocking is that it is very ambiguous even in Jesus' teaching. Jesus' sayings reveal that his message was not about the coming of the messiah. His preaching focused on the coming of God's kingdom, not the kingdom of the messiah. Jesus appears never to have proclaimed himself to be the messiah. He apparently rejected Peter's confession that he was the Christ by saying that Peter's idea was Satanic (Mark 8:27-33).

Furthermore, the disciples never asked Jesus about his views on the messiah. Before his crucifixion in the year 30 C.E., they were apparently not preoccupied with any speculations about a messiah. Messiah is a term that is fixed on Jesus during the passion narrative. It has to do with the inscription on the cross mostly, and it sticks afterward in an ironic way when the believers feel that he has survived death.

Let me be a bit more specific about this. According to the Gospel tradition, the inscription on the cross was "Jesus of Nazareth, the King of the Jews" (John 19:19). This has every chance of being accurate, because the church has no real interest in portraying Jesus as king of the Jews, when he is so much more. Furthermore, the Jews are pictured realistically reacting to the charge with the indignation that such a calumny would have occasioned: Write instead that he said he was king of the Jews (John 19:21). Does that mean that the title "Jesus of Nazareth, the King of the Jews" was entirely the product of an ironic charge brought against Jesus? Not entirely. Jesus' mission may have occasioned a great deal of messianic interest, as we have seen. But the words of Jesus himself are surprisingly suspicious of any such claim. Furthermore, any such ordinary messianic expectations of Jesus died with him. "We thought he was the one to redeem us" (Luke 24:21), say the utterly heartbroken disciples.

The most important passage from the Hebrew Bible that is quoted in the New Testament is Psalm 110, which the New Testament often cites in combination with Daniel 7:13, the prophecy of the son of man who is enthroned next to God. In it, God addresses the davidic king, calling him up to his throne: "The Lord says to my Lord: Sit at my right hand until I make your enemies your footstool" (Ps 110:1). God addresses his messiah as "My Lord." The passage does not prophesy a risen messiah or a suffering messiah or anything of the sort; the application to Christianity could not have been predicted ahead of time. Nothing in the Christian application of the passage from Psalm 110 is understandable without prior knowledge of the events of Easter Sunday accepted as fact by the Christian community. Furthermore, the passage does not prophesy anything about a future messiah. Instead, it specifically explains the significance of the empty tomb. This is very important to note: The process is typically Jewish but the exegesis is itself entirely novel because the events were entirely unexpected.

Now let's look at the second part of this passage. The most important idea implied in the reinterpretation of Psalm 110 is the divinity of the two figures, "God" and "My Lord." Lord is a term by which the Jews designated God. In Hebrew, the word Lord for God is different from but extremely close to the ordinary word Lord. One is *Adonai* and the other is *Adoni*. When translated into Greek or Aramaic, the two terms become one. In Christianity, and probably on the basis of passages like this (Ps 110:1), the Greek word *Kyrios*, meaning Lord, became a term describing not God himself, as in Judaism, but Christ. Thus, the earliest Christian exegesis already asserted the divinity of the figure of Jesus on the basis of his heavenly ascent and exaltation in Psalm 110.

Why should his followers have immediately jumped to the conclusion that Jesus had been resurrected? We can never know for sure because we shall never know precisely what was seen on Easter morning. We know that the Judaism of Jesus' day did not universally believe in resurrection. It was greatly debated. We moderns tend to underestimate this debate because the two surviving sects from the time of Jesus—Pharisaic–rabbinic Judaism and Christianity—both accept resurrection as fundamental to their beliefs. It is conceivable that the majority of Judea did not, even in the time of Jesus.

The one thing that can be shown is that where Jews did believe in resurrection, the occasion was almost always martyrdom. Resurrection makes its first clear appearance in the Maccabean Revolt, where it is held up as the reward for those who die for keeping God's law exactly and not abandoning it. Remember the prophecy of Daniel in this regard:

> Those who sleep in the dust will arise, some to everlasting reward and some to contempt. And those who are wise shall shine with the brightness of the heaven, like the stars forever (Dan 12:2-3).

Jesus ascends to heaven because astral immortality is promised to those martyrs who make others wise, and Jesus is preeminently a martyr. But Jesus' divinity is more complex than merely the identification with a divine name in the Psalms. Jesus' identification with the heavenly figure of the Son of man in Daniel 7 is crucial in understanding why the early Christians interpreted Jesus' ascension to have implied his divinity as well.

Because Jesus is also identified with the Son of man (perhaps he used the term of himself in his mission but what he meant by it we do not know), we know that he was not merely the first of those to be resurrected at the end of time.

The Son of man is but one name for a figure of extreme importance to Jewish mysticism in the first century. There was in the Bible a human theophany, a human appearance of God, often called the angel of the Lord but also called the *Kavod,* God's Glory, or even once the Son of man, as in Daniel. By the time of Jesus, these peculiar notions could be combined into a single, divine, human figure who carries or embodies the name of God. The best shorthand way to explain what the scriptural interpretations make of this figure is to call it God's principal angel, because that's what we call human manifestations of God in heaven. But this angel is not merely one of God's creatures. It participates in God's name somehow. It is this figure whom the Christians identified as Jesus, thus making the Christ and the Lord one.

Proof of this comes from Paul, who almost explicitly says that he identifies the mystical *Kavod*, God's Glory, with Jesus, the crucified messiah:

> For what we preach is not ourselves, but Jesus Christ as Lord, with ourselves as your servants for Jesus' sake. For it is the God who said, "Let light shine out of darkness," who has shone in our hearts to give the light of the knowledge of the glory of the Lord in the face of Christ (2 Cor 4:6).

This is not a simple statement that the face of Christ is glorious. It is a confession that Paul has himself seen the *Kavod*, God's glory, just as Ezekiel did. And this *Kavod* had the features and face of Jesus. (I don't know whether the vision came to Paul on the road to Damascus or from elsewhere among Paul's many visions; but the identification is surely to have been made by a visionary appearance of the Christ to him; see Acts 9:1-22; 22:4-16; 26:9-18.)

Furthermore, it is not just that Jesus is or has become part of God. Those who believe in him will also become divine, just as Enoch was transformed into the Son of man. All of this is the subjective confession of the fulfillment of Daniel's prophecy that those who are wise will shine like the stars, for angels and stars are one in the Bible. Paul tells us just what the process feels like. It is absorption into the Son of man, *summorphosis*—not the pale "becoming like him" of the ordinary English translation but the more dramatic

Greek meaning of being remade together into the form and shape of the Glory, as Paul expresses it.

Are there precedents for this belief in Judaism, before Christianity? Yes. When we look carefully at the beliefs of the first century, we discover that many, many Jews were willing to posit that some ordinary human beings were divine. Philo, who was an orthodox Jew in practice, thought that Moses became divine when he ascended Mount Sinai. The Dead Sea sectarians thought that the leader of the angelic forces of good, whom they sometimes called Melchisedek, was the creature called *elohim* in Psalm 82. Some Jews believed that God had a principal angel, named *Yahoel* (or *Metatron*, later) who carried or personified the name of God. He might even be called *YHWH* Junior. So there were lots of Jews who thought that God could be divided into two different figures, an old and a young one (Dan 7:9-13).

But were there any who identified this figure with a historical figure who was once in their midst and to whom they now offered prayers for the forgiveness of sins? No! In spite of all the precedents (and they are many and interesting, but time and space do not suffice to tell all about them), the Christian explanation of the empty tomb was unique. Although angels may have served as bearers of prayers and as intercessors for humans (e.g., Tob. 12:11-15), God is the object of prayers by humans and angels alike. Christianity is the first or at least the most important early exception to the rule; it is what Larry Hurtado[5] has called an important new mutation. The Christian methods of interpreting scripture, however, the way in which these ideas were justified, were gleaned from all the Jewish groups during this period.

This does not imply the agreement of the unconvinced parts of the Jewish community. There is some important evidence that it was just exactly this one point, praying to the second power in heaven, which accounted for half of the Jewish resistance to, let us call it, the Christian interpretation of Israel's traditions. Jesus felt that these mystical and complex traditions compromised monotheism, especially as the Christians not only posited the existence of this creature but offered prayers to Jesus as Christ as if to a god. There is a good deal of evidence that Judaism criticized early Christianity for being dualist, "those who say that there are two powers in heaven." The other arm of Jewish resistance to Christianity, its antinomianism or freedom from the laws set down in the Torah, was the other great issue but it must remain for another time.

Take a long view of Christianity and realize it is but one of a number of Jewish sects that saw the signs of the times and with great fear and trembling proclaimed that the messiah, the person who would fulfill the destiny of Israel, had arrived. The process continues into this century. We can expect Jews and Gentiles to react the same way with the approaching end of the millennium.

Take, for example, the little Jewish town, a *Stetl*, in far Transylvania that was so isolated that it feared that the messiah might come without their knowing it. So they hired the town beggar to stand on a high platform and watch for the coming of the messiah.

After he had been working for a while, the townspeople asked him how he liked the job. He replied:

"You know, it's uncomfortable to be so high above everyone. And sometimes it's lonely. And of course the pay is low. But the job security is terrific." The same is true for college professors—it's lonely, the pay is low, but the job security is terrific. And unlike the town beggar, I can sit down so I will.

For Discussion

1. Why must one first understand the similarities and differences between Christianity and Judaism in order to really understand how Christianity arose from Judaism?

2. Did Judean society have a fixed concept of a messiah?

3. Did Jesus want the term "messiah" applied to him? Does the New Testament apply the title to him? Explain.

4. Did Jews in Jesus' time who believed in the resurrection connect it with martyrdom? If so, how did Christians appropriate this understanding and apply it to Jesus?

5. What is the relationship of the title Son of man to messiah, to Jesus, and to the Christian interpretation of who he is?

6. What accounted for half of the Jewish resistance to the Jesus movement? Did Judaism criticize early Christianity for being dualistic?

7. From reading this chapter, what new insights and understandings do you have about the concept of messiah and its use in Judaism and Christianity?

8

FROM CHRIST TO GOD:
THE CHRISTIAN PERSPECTIVE

MONIKA K. HELLWIG

◼

That such a topic as this can be raised in such a forum as this gives witness to the great progress that has been made in mutual trust and respect between Jewish and Christian scholars. The increasing collaboration has greatly enriched us all in scholarship, in piety, and in efforts toward social justice in our world. Although there have been many initiatives of this kind, the progress made has been due not least but very substantially to the Center for Jewish–Christian Learning, at the University of St. Thomas. It is a privilege to participate in the Jay Phillips Symposium of the Center.

The question of what is meant by the divinity claim that Christians make for Jesus is central to Christian self-understanding. In the theological reflection and debate over this issue in the course of the centuries, not enough attention has been paid to the Judaic origins of the claim. As Professor Segal has so insightfully and helpfully described and analyzed, the divinity claim did not originate with gentile followers of Jesus but with his early Jewish friends and followers who experienced the indescribable event we name the resurrection, as they themselves named it out of their intertestamental tradition. What emerges very clearly in the early centuries of Christianity, however, is that a divinity claim for a human individual has a very wide variety of meanings for people according to the cultural and religious—and, in some cases, philosophical—background that they bring to it. There is, for instance, an immense gulf between two well-known early statements, one Jewish and the other gentile. In chapter two of the Acts of the Apostles in the New Testament, Peter concludes his long sermon to fellow Jews, in which he has repeatedly cited prophetic texts and Psalms from the Hebrew Scriptures to illustrate their forward thrust of expectation, with the sentence: "Therefore let the entire house of Israel know with certainty that God has made him both Lord and Messiah, this Jesus whom you crucified."[1] There are clearly two named in this claim: God and Jesus. God acts and Jesus is recipient of the action. The action of God for Jesus as expressed by Peter clearly parallels the action of God described by Psalm 110: "The Lord says to my lord, 'Sit at my right hand until I make your enemies your footstool'" (Ps 110:1).

In this statement of Peter, echoing the Psalm, there is respect for mystery. God remains transcendent and is seen in contrast to Jesus who was crucified and has been raised and is exalted and in some unspecified sense drawn into the divinity. In contrast, one of the earliest gentile statements of the same claim is that of Ignatius of Antioch. Although he also clearly indicates relationship rather than identity between "God the Father" and the "Son," his opening greeting in his letter to the Romans ends: "To those who in flesh and spirit are at one with his every command, filled with the grace of God without distraction, and strained clear from every extraneous pollution, abundant greetings of unalloyed joy in *Jesus Christ our God*" (italics added).[2] The simple naming of Jesus as "our God" is something of an entirely different order from the nuanced statement of Peter cited above. And this is really where the serious and apparently intractable difficulties in Christology begin—in a simplification in gentile context and language of the elusive and allusive Hebrew way of speaking about the mystery of God and of God's dealings with creation and history.

The shaping of the classic Christology of the Councils and of subsequent Christian tradition was no easy matter but was fraught with bitter controversy, misunderstandings, and confusion. The early lack of nuance on the one hand and of precision on the other led authors like Athenagoras of Athens to try to explain the divinity claim in terms intelligible to Greek intellectuals. Insisting first on the absolute unity and spirituality of God, Athenagoras poses the question to his second-century contemporaries, whether there is any intelligibility in the claim that God has a son but that this does not imply a plurality of gods. To which he replies by allusion to Greek philosophy that the statement becomes intelligible when it is understood that the sonship referred to is not a biological sonship but the being begotten of a thought or utterance.[3] The notion of "logos" as the mediating principle between the utterly inaccessible ultimate one and the world of plurality and contingency (the ordering principle of the plurality) was familiar. At the same time, Athenagoras is in the tradition of the prologue of John's Gospel in using the term logos allusively to imply an equation with the speaking of God in the creation narrative of Genesis 1.

This way of dealing with the divinity claim had obvious advantages of preserving the unity of God as well as the mystery of the divinity claim for Jesus. It was not entirely lost but it did gradually give way to another mode of explanation in which the personhood or fundamental identity of Jesus was transferred outside history and creation into eternity and divinity. This seems to occur clearly for the first time (at least in the extant documents) in Origen's *Peri Archon* (*De Principiis*), where the identity of Jesus is established in the eternally preexisting Word before any account is presented of

Jesus in history.[4] However, for Origen, only God the Father is in the strictest sense God, giving Origen a subordinationist Christology and Trinitarian theology which the churches later rejected. What the churches did not reject in Origen's understanding was the introduction of the vocabulary of three Persons (*hypostases*) existing from or in eternity. This has a rather different meaning in Origen's subordinationist view from the meaning carried in the later non-subordinationist Trinitarian orthodoxy.

While western theology of the early ages appears to have been more dogged in its emphasis on monotheism, both Hippolytus and Tertullian in the early third century acknowledge plurality as in some way intrinsic to God, as for instance in the inclusion of word and wisdom, or of power and counsel (reminiscent of Hebraic stories in which God consults with his Torah and his wisdom).[5] Tertullian introduced the term *trinitas*, which has gained almost universal acceptance among Christian communities since that time. But Tertullian insisted that the distinction made did not imply division. It is Tertullian also who insisted, and was later widely quoted to that effect, that when Christians claim that Jesus is divine and human they mean just that, both properly divine (in contrast to the qualified statement of his contemporary, Origen) and properly human, not a mixture or *tertium quid* (third something or other). The language of *persona* and *substantia* (later, *natura*) was really established at this time, although bitter, and sometimes venomous, debates over the appropriate use of Greek equivalents continued through the fourth and earlier fifth centuries in the writings and *viva voce* arguments surrounding the great Councils.

The question may well be asked as to why the issue kept recurring. The answer seems to be in the maxim, *lex orandi lex credendi*. What people were reciting in their worship was to them the rule of faith, but it was difficult not to see it as inconsistent. They were professing faith in the one God of Israel, but they were also praying to Jesus as divine and they were reciting trinitarian doxologies that praised and adored Father, Son, and Spirit equally. Sooner or later, a systematic exigence was bound to be felt to harmonize the discordant elements in the formulation of faith.

It was, however, the emerging predominance of the personal model for the preexistence of Jesus that led to the most difficult questions—questions that would not have arisen had we been able to remain within the bounds of such models or analogies as word of God, Wisdom, light from light, life from life, retaining the term Son of God for the historical Jesus. With heavy emphasis on the personal model, Arius of Alexandria was led at the beginning of the fourth century to insist explicitly on Origen's subordinationism of the previous century, troubling his own and other bishops and leading to the Council of Nicea in 325, reinforced later by the Council of Constantinople in 381. The Councils defined that Jesus, son of Mary, is of one substance with the Father, God from God. Lest there continue to be any doubt of the identification made in the Niceno-Constantinopolitan Creed, the Council of Ephesus in 431 insisted that it is the one Jesus of whom we speak when attributing both divine and human characteristics. The Council of Chalcedon in 451 canonized the existing statements to that effect, adding the symmetry that Jesus is "of one substance with the Father as to his divinity, and of one substance with us as to his humanity."[6] The Chalcedonian documents and formula have remained the touchstone of orthodoxy for most Christian churches ever since that time.

It has been widely acknowledged among contemporary theologians of the western (Latin-derived) churches that the language with which we are left is troublesome and misleading. Many have not hesitated to apply the term tritheism to the way trinitarian doctrine is commonly understood. It is readily acknowledged that the simple transliteration of Tertullian's term *persona* (for the conciliar Greek *hypostasis*) is seriously flawed because the modern concept of person as an individual reflexive self-awareness and center of spontaneity is simply not what was intended by the term either when

Tertullian introduced it or when the Councils adopted it in defining orthodoxy. However, such observations on the part of theologians have not significantly affected the teaching in the churches, because church leaders have on the whole clung to verbal orthodoxy as seeming safer. They have found reassurance in repeating the same words and have not readily acknowledged that the phenomenon of semantic shift (the changing meaning of words) could affect official church formulations and render them very fragile. For the major church traditions, it has been a conciliar–dogmatic fundamentalism rather than a biblical fundamentalism that has endangered intelligibility and coherence.

However, even among those intellectuals who are willing to acknowledge that the term "person" is misleading today and must be subjected to textual and contextual hermeneutics, there is a common reluctance to face the more fundamental question of whether the enterprise of the great councils was flawed in its intellectual conception. The question arises whether a clarity, comprehension, and precision were being sought which by their very nature are alien to religious discourse. And this I take to be a characteristically Judaic question from which theological development in the Christian church might have profited had the separation of the two traditions not been so fierce from early times, and had the Judeo-Christians not been excluded and suppressed. There are, then, some penetrating questions to be asked about Christology which are most relevant to the Jewish–Christian dialogue, and there is at this time in theological history a new opening to discuss them. The biblical and intertestamentary heritage common to Christians and Jews involved a respect for mystery—and an intellectual humility before it—which was largely implicit. The judicious use of narrative, symbolism, discreet allusion, paradox, and so forth, was an implicit acknowledgment of the nature and limitations of religious language and of faith assertions. The Christian option for Greek philosophical categories in patristic times and for intensively philosophical systematization

142

of the religious heritage in medieval times did much to weaken that acknowledgment. But modern philosophy itself has taken relentless (one might say merciless) note of the nature and limitation of all language, the relation of religious language to truth claims, the role of symbol in human understanding and expression, the troubled question of relation between subject and object in knowledge, and so forth. What that does for Christology is that it opens a window of opportunity to reconsider the traditional doctrinal formulations, asking some radical epistemological questions and relating them to the contexts and arguments that shaped the historical development of the doctrines.

In that light, how are we to interpret the classic formulations of the Councils? In the first place, cautiously. As frequently pointed out *viva voce* by the late Bernard Lonergan, careful study of writings of those Church Fathers most involved in the debates[7] shows that even such central terms as "nature" and "person" are sometimes used in a reversal of their meanings in the course of a struggle to come to formulation in which all are floundering and many would have preferred a less definitional and more suggestive approach. In any case, the resultant formula, seen in the context of the debates, looks rather like the algebraic trick for dealing with too much complexity or obscurity: "Let X and Y equal the two unknowns." There is no doubt that more comprehension and clarity was often assumed in subsequent theological discussion of the conciliar formulas than those present and voting saw or intended.

A second suggestion on how to interpret the conciliar dogmatic heritage is to note and bring back into play the alternation of personal and impersonal titles for Jesus. There is a tendency in the earlier literature to use personal titles such as Son of God and the heavily allusive Son of man for the human, historical Jesus, and to use the impersonal such as Word, Light, Wisdom, Image for the divine preexistence. This is underscored when the human Jesus, both in his historical existence and in his liturgical mediation, is depicted

as praying to the Father. It would seem that this is not merely an interesting point to note about the past, but the golden thread through
the maze of contemporary dogmatic accumulation.

A third suggestion as to how to interpret the conciliar formulations of the divinity claim for Jesus is to note the continuity as well
as the discontinuity between what is said of Jesus in the early Christian writings and liturgies and what is said of the human person as
such and of the follower of Jesus in particular. More especially in
the eastern (Greek-derived) church tradition, the concept of deifi-
cation or divinization of the believer has been a continuous thread.
In both eastern and western thought, the image that Irenaeus
picked up from the biblical creation stories is honored: that the
glory of God is the full coming to life of the human person. It is not
strange to find the assertion that the human person as such, every
human person, is an Image of God, a Word of God, reflection of the
Light of God, expression of the Wisdom of God. The awareness of
this continuity in what is said of Adam, of every person, and of Jesus, would seem to be a very helpful corrective for a style of Christology that is based too much on the way we know and think about
things rather than *people,* and that simply claims too much for the
power of human knowledge and language.

This essay has dealt so far (and all too briefly) with what happened in the development of dogmatic Christology, and with some
thoughts about the interpretation of the formulas the Councils left
us. A third aspect that may be helpful in the context of Jewish–
Christian dialogue is the question of why the authoritative definition of the divinity of Jesus was and is a matter of such importance
for Christians. How important it was in the fourth and fifth centuries is clear from some of the memories that Church Fathers
recorded in their writings from their time at the Councils: One
could not get a pair of sandals repaired without getting into an argument with the cobbler over exact Christological terminology; the
monks came down from the mountains with cudgels to defend

Mary's right to the title "bearer of God," and so forth. Christian writers from Athanasius in the fourth century to Anselm in the late eleventh century were at pains to explain that if Jesus is not divine, then we have no guarantee that we are redeemed. They explained this in different ways, according to the analogies on which they were able to draw in their particular human and social contexts, but they are at one about the assertion. To Jewish observers, this must seem quite strange as God can redeem through whatever means God chooses: the making of a covenant, the giving of the Law, the sending of the prophets, disasters calling people to conversion, and so forth. The clearly gentile argument, coming from a world of plurality of cultures and prior religious traditions, is that there must be a special, indeed a unique reason for unconditional trust in the way of Jesus. In a variant form, once the death of Jesus is seen as redemptive, it must have a unique value quite unlike any other noble and self-sacrificing death.[8] It should be noted that the same writers who are most insistent in making the redemption dependent on the divinity of Christ are equally insistent that the redemption would not be a reality if Jesus were not fully and truly human. The argument is twofold here: (1) if Jesus were not truly human, he could not be a new Adam, with a headship gathering the corporate being of humanity and able to share with all others the renewed intimacy with God he himself had: and (2) if Jesus were not authentically human, he could not rightly speak for or act for the human community in its encounter with God. This became, at times in the history of Christian theology, almost a mathematical equation of trying to balance the infinite alienation with the finite resources to bridge it and finding the resources wanting unless there was an intervention of infinite proportion.

What this Christian preoccupation is probably becomes clearer when seen in parallel with foundations of Jewish identity and hope. The latter have been expressed in terms of the city of Jerusalem, the Temple, and the Land; in terms of covenant, election, and Law; in terms of the patriarchs, the Exodus, and the promise of the World to Come—all long supported by peoplehood resting on natural bonds of blood relationship as well as bonds of cultural continuity that supply a certain underlying matter-of-factness to Jewish identity in its relationship to God as well as in all other ways. Christian identity is other than this, having ultimately only one anchor—the person of Jesus. The Christian awareness of relationship to God—and, more importantly perhaps, the Christian assurance of favorable relationship to God—rests on one point of guarantee that the whole enterprise is authentic, and that point is the person of Jesus of Nazareth. So much is this the case that in Christian theology it has been axiomatic to say that Jesus is not simply one who relays God's revelation to his followers: he *is* the self-revelation of the divine. At its simplest, therefore, the Christian claim for the divinity of Jesus is the claim that we meet the one true God than whom there is no other, when we meet Jesus. The glory, or revelation, of God is in the human person fully alive, and the Christian community claims to have seen that human person fully alive in whom the divine glory is revealed and personified. Moreover, the earliest friends and followers of Jesus saw Israel's witness function to the nations coming to a point of definition in Jesus—the merits and fidelity of his ancestors and his people coming to a certain fruition in him.

Such contemporary rephrasing of what we mean by the divinity claim for Jesus may leave some more thoughtful and pertinacious Jewish thinkers with the question as to what, then, we mean by asserting a trinity in God that is not simply in the relationship of God to us in history but is asserted to be in the very being of God. The first thing to be noted is that we have the same semantic drift problem in the use of the term person (*hypostasis, persona*) in the fixed and firm dogmatic formulations relating to the faith in a triune God. How early in our history that became problematic is evident from the so-called Athanasian Creed. Originating possibly as early as the late fifth century, it set out at considerable length in what respects and characteristics God is to be understood as threefold and in what characteristics the unity is to be strictly maintained. How difficult such a process has been is evident in the observed fact, mentioned before, that there is no doubt that triunity in God is commonly popularly translated into tritheism. It is true that this quasi-Christian brand of polytheism is a considerable improvement on some of those polytheist traditions against which Israel of old struggled so persistently, because these three do not fight with one another, nor do they take partisan positions on behalf of particular nations leaving others to find their own gods to defend them. However, introducing plurality into God negates the meaning of the term and has many unhealthy consequences. It has been suggested repeatedly, therefore, in contemporary Christian theology that the word "person" be substituted by one less easily misunderstood in this context. So far this has been quite unsuccessful because of the preoccupation with verbal orthodoxy at all costs among official church leaders. All alternatives suggested seem to have some linguistic link with positions rejected as heretical in the ancient church—alternatives such as three modes or ways or faces. In fact, the earlier Christian Church Fathers wrote of the triune God only in terms of God's relationship to us in history. But gradually, as Greek philosophical categories became more pervasive, the "really real" was seen as necessarily timeless. By the principle of *lex orandi lex credendi*, Christian thinkers felt compelled to be consistent with the liturgical formulas which so frequently addressed Father, Son, and Spirit, One God. If that is a true representation of God, then it must be what God is in eternity, intrinsically or essentially, so to speak.

What then is the contemporary thoughtful and well-informed Christian to make of this? In the first place, it is clear that it is an impertinence of staggering proportions that we should claim to scrutinize and define the divine; in this relationship, we do not grasp but are grasped, we do not watch but are watched, we do not understand but are understood. What this realization effectively does is to bring us back to those early Church Fathers who claimed no more than that they were reflecting on and marveling at the wonderful encounters with the divine in history, and thanking and praising the God who had so graciously revealed something of the divine in those encounters. What may be said beyond this about the trinitarian formulations is simply this: we acknowledge and profess that God truly is as shown or self-revealed in those encounters, because with God there can be no deceit. Therefore, we are sure that God is indeed the one source and guiding providence of all that is, and that in Jesus we have met that caring providence and compassion,[9] which also sustains us as the breath of God in the community of believers. We are sure that in all this it is the one God that we encounter, the real God than whom there is no other.

For Discussion

1. How did Ignatius of Antioch, Athenagoras of Athens, Origen, Tertullian, and Arius of Alexandria attempt to explain the divinity claims about Jesus and his relationship to the one God?

2. How did the ecumenical councils of Nicea, Constantinople, Ephesus, and Chalcedon wrestle with and make sense out of the divinity claims about Jesus?

3. What are the various suggestions offered in the chapter for interpreting the conciliar formulas of the divinity claim for Jesus? State, and react to each suggestion.

4. Is redemption dependent on the divinity or the humanity of Jesus or both?

5. How does the Jewish relationship to God differ from the Christian relationship to God, and what is the pivotal role of Jesus in the Christian view?

6. React to the statement: Christians are tritheists.

7. Why is it impertinent for anyone to claim that he or she has the ability to scrutinize and define the divine?

8. From reading this chapter, what new insights and/or understandings do you have about the early Church's understandings of God and its claims about Jesus' divinity?

CONTRIBUTORS

Shaye J. D. Cohen is the Ungerleider Professor of Judaic Studies at Brown University. He received his bachelor's degree from Yeshiva College, rabbinic ordination from the Jewish Theological Seminary, and a Ph.D. from Columbia University. He is the author of *From the Maccabees to the Mishnah*, coeditor, with Edward Greenstein, of *The State of Jewish Studies*, and author of numerous studies on the history of Judaism.

John R. Donahue, S.J. is professor of New Testament at the Jesuit School of Theology and Graduate Theological Union at Berkeley. He holds six academic degrees with a Ph.D. in New Testament from the University of Chicago. He was President of the Catholic Biblical Association of America (1993–1994) and has served as associate editor of the *Catholic Biblical Quarterly*. He is the author of *The Gospel in Parable: Metaphor, Narrative, and Theology in the Synoptic Gospels* and *Are You The Christ? The Trial Narrative of the Gospel of Mark*.

Paula Fredriksen is the William Goodman Aurelio Professor of the Appreciation of Scripture at Boston University. She holds a diploma in Theology from Oxford University and a Ph.D. from Princeton University in History of Religions. An editor for *Studies in Christianity and Judaism*, she also sits on the steering committee of the Historical Jesus section in the American Academy of Religion. Her most recent book, *From Jesus to Christ: The Origins of the New Testament Images of Jesus*, won the 1988 Governors' award for Best Book from Yale University Press. Awarded the Lady Davis Professorship in 1994, she has also taught ancient Christianity in the religion department of the Hebrew University, Jerusalem.

Monika K. Hellwig is the Landegger Distinguished Professor of Theology at Georgetown University. She received both an M.A. and a Ph.D. from Catholic University of America as well as 12 honorary doctorates. She served as President of the Catholic Theological Society of America (1986–1987) and is the recipient of both the Marianist Award for her contribution to American Catholic Scholarship, and the Catholic University Award for Outstanding Achievement in the field of Religion. She is the author of nineteen books, her more recent being *Jesus: The Compassion of God* and *Catholic Faith and Contemporary Questions.*

Anthony J. Saldarini is Professor of Theology at Boston College. He holds a Ph.D. from Yale University and is the recipient of numerous grants from learned organizations. He is the author of seven books, including *Pharisees, Scribes and Sadducees in Palestinian Society; Jesus and Passover;* and *Matthew's Christian-Jewish Community;* and the section on "Jewish History and Literature of the Greco-Roman Period" in the *Cambridge Bible Companion.*

E. P. Sanders is Arts and Sciences Professor of Religion at Duke University. He holds doctoral degrees from Oxford University and the University of Helsinki. Before coming to Duke he held positions at McMaster University and the University of Oxford. An expert on Jesus and Paul and the times in which they lived, his publications include *Paul and Palestinian Judaism, Jesus and Judaism,* and *Judaism: Practice and Belief.* Since 1990, he has chaired the Seminar on the Historical Jesus of the Society of New Testament Studies. He is a Fellow of the British Academy.

Lawrence H. Schiffman is Professor of Hebrew and Judaic Studies and Near Eastern Languages and Literatures at New York University's Skirball Department of Hebrew and Judaic Studies. He holds a Ph.D. from Brandeis University and is a specialist in the Dead Sea Scrolls, Judaism in Late Antiquity, and the history of Jewish law and Talmudic literature. He was featured in the PBS Nova Series "Secrets of the Dead Sea Scrolls." He has written eight books and numerous scholarly articles. Among these are *Sectarian Law in the Dead Sea Scrolls, Who Was a Jew?*, *Rabbinic Perspectives on the Jewish–Christian Schism*, and *Archaeology and History in the Dead Sea Scrolls*.

Alan F. Segal is Professor of Religion at Barnard College–Columbia University. He received a Ph.D. from Yale University. He has held fellowships from the Guggenheim Foundation, the Woodrow Wilson Foundation, the Council of Learned Societies, and the National Endowment for the Humanities. Among his published books are such titles as *Rebecca's Children: Judaism and Christianity in the Roman World*, *The Other Judaism of Late Antiquity*, *Two Powers in Heaven*, and *Paul the Convert: The Apostasy and Apostolate of Saul of Tarsus*.

Max A. Shapiro is the Director of the Center for Jewish–Christian Learning at the University of St. Thomas in St. Paul, Minnesota, and Rabbi Emeritus of Temple Israel, Minneapolis, Minnesota. He holds degrees from Clark University, a D.Ed. from the University of Cincinnati, and honorary doctorates from Hebrew Union College–Jewish Institute of Religion and from the University of St. Thomas. He wrote, compiled, and edited a number of liturgical volumes, contributed articles to various publications, and is the author of *Here I Am; Send Me*. Under his leadership as the first Director of the

Center for Jewish–Christian Learning, the Center has become nationally and internationally known as a place where Christians and Jews can come together in ecumenical dialogue. He was ordained a Rabbi from Hebrew Union College.

Arthur E. Zannoni is a free-lance writer and consultant in the areas of biblical studies and Jewish–Christian Relations. From 1985 to 1991, he taught on the faculty of the Saint Paul Seminary School of Divinity of the University of St. Thomas, and served as Associate Director of its Center for Jewish–Christian Learning. In addition to numerous articles, he is coeditor, with Michael Shermis, of *Introduction to Jewish–Christian Relations* and author of *The Old Testament: A Bibliography*. He is the recipient of the Temple Israel (Minneapolis) Interreligious Award for his work in promoting interfaith dialogue. In 1994 he won the first place award from the Catholic Press Association for his article "Jesus the Jew" published in the national newsletter *Catholic Update*.

ABBREVIATIONS

AB	*Anchor Bible*
ABD	*Anchor Bible Dictionary*
ʿAbod. Zar.	ʿ*Aboda Zara*
Ag. Ap.	*Against Apion* (Josephus)
Ant.	*Jewish Antiquities* (Josephus)
ANRW	*Aufsteig und Niedergang der römischen Welt*
BAR	*Biblical Archaeologist Reader*
BJS	Brown Judaic Studies
CBQ	*Catholic Biblical Quarterly*
CD	*Covenant of Damascus*
C.E.	Common Era
Ep. Arist.	*Epistle of Aristeas*
HTR	*Harvard Theological Review*
IDB	*Interpreter's Dictionary of the Bible*, G. A. Buttrick (ed.)
Int	*Interpretation*

JJS	*Journal of Jewish Studies*
JSNTSup	Journal for the Study of the New Testament—Supplement Series
JSOTSup	Journal for the Study of the Old Testament—Supplement Series
JTS	*Journal of Theological Studies*
*JTS*NS	Journal of Theological Studies, New Series
J.W.	*Jewish War* (Josephus)
NJBC	*The New Jerome Biblical Commentary*, R. E. Brown et al. (eds.)
NovT	*Novum Testamentum*
NovTSup	Novum Testamentum, Supplements
NRSV	New Revised Standard Version
NTS	*New Testament Studies*
Pss. Sol.	*Psalms of Solomon*
Q	Synoptic Sayings Source (material common to Matthew and Luke, but not found in Mark)
1QpHab	*Pesher on Habakkuk* from Qumran Cave 1
1QS	*Serek hayyahad (Rule of the Community, Manual of Discipline)*
RSV	Revised Standard Version
SBLDS	SBL Dissertation Series
SBLSP	SBL Seminar Papers
SBT	Studies in Biblical Theology

SCJ	Studies in Christianity and Judaism
SJ	Studia judaica
SJLA	Studies in Judaism in Late Antiquity
SNTSMS	Society for New Testament Studies Monograph Series
SPB	Studia postbiblica
ZNW	*Zeitschrift für die neutestamentliche Wissenschaft*

NOTES

CHAPTER 1   JUDAISM AT THE TIME OF JESUS

1. In preparing this text for publication, I have maintained the format and tone of the lecture on which it is based. To keep the text clean, I have omitted notes; scholarly documentation can be found in the standard textbooks.

CHAPTER 2   PLURALISM OF PRACTICE AND BELIEF IN FIRST-CENTURY JUDAISM

1. For Galilee as a distinct region, see Sean Freyne, *Galilee from Alexander the Great to Hadrian, 323 B.C.E. to 135 C.E.: A Study of Second Temple Judaism* (Wilmington: Glazier/Notre Dame: University of Notre Dame, 1980), and Lee I. Levine, ed., *The Galilee in Late Antiquity* (New York: Jewish Theological Seminary, 1992).

2. For the slow growth of rabbinic Judaism, see Lee I. Levine, *The Rabbinic Class of Roman Palestine in Late Antiquity* (New York: Jewish Theological Seminary/Jerusalem: Yad Izhak Ben-Zvi, 1989), and Martin Goodman, *State and Society in Roman Galilee, A.D. 132–212* (Totowa, N.J.: Rowman and Allanheld, 1983) p. 3.

3. For studies of diaspora Judaism, see Judith Lieu et al., eds., *The Jews among Pagans and Christians in the Roman Empire* (London: Routledge, 1992); E. Schürer, G. Vermes, et al., *The History of the Jewish People in the Age of Jesus Christ (175 B.C.–A.D. 135)* (4 vols.; Edinburgh: T. & T. Clark, 1973–87) 3:1–176; Jack N. Lightstone, *The Commerce of the Sacred: Mediation of the Divine among Jews in the*

Graeco-Roman Diaspora (BJS 59; Chico, Calif.: Scholars Press, 1984), and *Society, the Sacred, and Scripture in Ancient Judaism: A Sociology of Knowledge* (SCJ 3; Ontario: Wilfred J. Laurier University Press, 1988); Louis H. Feldman, *Jew and Gentile in the Ancient World: Attitudes and Interactions from Alexander to Justinian* (Princeton: Princeton University Press, 1993).

4. Bezalel Porten, *Archives from Elephantine: The Life of an Ancient Jewish Military Colony* (Berkeley: University of California, 1968).

5. H. J. Leon, *The Jews of Ancient Rome* (Philadelphia: Jewish Publication Society, 1960).

6. For the cultural setting of Galilee and the importance of regionalism, see Eric M. Meyers and James F. Strange, *Archaeology, the Rabbis and Early Christianity* (Nashville: Abingdon, 1981) ch. 3.

7. Although some scholars argue for an urban–rural tension, villages and cities in Galilee were closely tied together. See Douglas Edwards, "The Socio-Economic and Cultural Ethos of the Lower Galilee in the First Century: Implications for the Nascent Jesus Movement," in Levine, *Galilee* 53–73; Sean Freyne, "Urban–Rural Relations in First-Century Galilee: Some Suggestions from the Literary Sources," ibid., 75–91; J. Andrew Overman, "Who Were the First Urban Christians? Urbanization in Galilee in the First Century," in David Lull, ed. (SBLSP; Atlanta: Scholars Press, 1988) 160–68.

8. For recent archaeological finds at Sepphoris, see Eric M. Meyers, "Roman Sepphoris in the Light of New Archaeological Evidence and Recent Research," in Levine, *Galilee* 321–38, and James F. Strange, "Six Campaigns at Sepphoris: The University of South Florida Excavations, 1983–89," ibid., 339–55.

9. For a sociological analysis of the structure of Jewish society in the Second Temple period, see Anthony J. Saldarini, *Pharisees, Scribes and Sadducees in Palestinian Society* (Wilmington: Glazier, 1988; Edinburgh: T. & T. Clark, 1989) chs. 3–4.

10. For the problem of debt in the first century C.E., see Martin Goodman, "The First Jewish Revolt: Social Conflict and the Problem of Debt," *JJS* 33 (1983) 417–27.

11. Most of the data come from the Jewish historian Flavius Josephus. For a convenient analysis of his material on social unrest, see Richard A. Horsley and John S. Hanson, *Bandits, Prophets and Messiahs: Popular Movements at the Time of Jesus* (Minneapolis: Winston, 1985).

12. For an introduction to apocalyptic literature, see John J. Collins, *The Apocalyptic Imagination: An Introduction to Apocalyptic Literature* (New York: Crossroad, 1984); M. E. Stone, "Apocalyptic Literature," in ibid., *Jewish Writings of the Second Temple Period* (Compendia Rerum Iudaicarum ad Novum Testamentum) II: 2 (Philadelphia: Fortress, 1984) 383–441.

13. For an emphasis on the revelatory nature of apocalypses, see Christopher Rowland, *The Open Heaven: A Study of Apocalyptic in Judaism and Early Christianity* (New York: Crossroad, 1982).

14. Much of Second Temple Jewish literature is collected in James H. Charlesworth, ed., *The Old Testament Pseudepigrapha* (2 vols.; Garden City: Doubleday, 1983–85).

15. For recent treatments of the Essenes and Dead Sea Scrolls, see Geza Vermes, *The Dead Sea Scrolls: Qumran in Perspective* (Philadelphia: Fortress, 1978); Devorah Dimat, "Qumran Sectarian Literature," in Stone, *Jewish Writings* 483–550; John J. Collins, "Essenes" (*ABD*; New York: Doubleday, 1992) 2: 619–26; Schürer, Vermes, *History* 3: 380–469.

16. For a sociological analysis of the Pharisees, see Saldarini, *Pharisees.*

17. The agenda of the Pharisees is best brought out by Jacob Neusner, *The Rabbinic Traditions about the Pharisees before 70* (3 vols.; Leiden: Brill, 1971); see also Neusner's popular summary, *From Politics to Piety: The Emergence of Pharisaic Judaism* (Englewood Cliffs, N.J.: Prentice-Hall, 1973).

18. For a critical analysis of the little that is said about the Sadducees in Josephus, the new Testament, and rabbinic literature, see Saldarini, *Pharisees,* and Gary Porton, "Sadducees," *ABD* 4: 892–95.

19. Josephus, *Life* 11–12.

20. For the complex evolution of the groups active in the war against Rome, see Horsley and Hanson, *Bandits,* and Jonathan

Price, *Jerusalem under Siege: The Collapse of the Jewish State 66–70 C.E.* (Brill's Series in Jewish Studies 3; Leiden: Brill, 1992).

21. For sects, see Bryan Wilson, *Magic and the Millennium: A Sociological Study of Religious Movements of Protest among Tribal and Third-World Peoples* (London: Heinemann, 1973); *Patterns of Sectarianism* (London: Heilmann, 1967). For deviance, a clear introduction is Stephen F. Pfohl, *Images of Deviance and Social Control: A Sociological History* (New York: McGraw-Hill, 1985), and Edwin H. Pfuhl, *The Deviance Process* (New York: Van Nostrand, 1980).

22. Edwin M. Schur, *The Politics of Deviance: Stigma Contests and the Uses of Power* (Englewood Cliffs, N.J.: Prentice-Hall, 1980). For an application of deviance to Matthew's community, see Anthony J. Saldarini, "The Gospel of Matthew and Jewish–Christian Conflict," in David Balch, ed., *Social History of the Matthean Community: Cross-Disciplinary Approaches* (Minneapolis: Fortress, 1991) 38–61, esp. 44–48.

23. The tension between deviance as destructive and as formative for society is brought out well by Nahman Ben-Yehuda, *Deviance and Moral Boundaries: Witchcraft, the Occult, Deviant Sciences and Scientists* (Chicago: University of Chicago Press, 1985) 1–20, esp. 3. On the positive effects of deviance, see Kai T. Ericson, *Wayward Puritans: A Study in the Sociology of Deviance* (New York: Wiley, 1966) 3–5.

24. For an analysis of the Gospel of Matthew as a Jewish book, see Anthony J. Saldarini, *Matthew's Christian–Jewish Community* (Chicago Studies in the History of Judaism; Chicago: University of Chicago Press, 1994).

25. The typology used here is found in Wilson, *Magic*.

CHAPTER 3   THE JEWISHNESS OF JESUS: COMMANDMENTS CONCERNING INTERPERSONAL RELATIONS

1. J. B. Soloveitchik, "Confrontation," *Tradition* 6:2 (1964) 5–29.

2. The literal meaning of Hebrew *ben ʾadam la-ḥavero* is "between one person and another."

3. L. H. Schiffman, *From Text to Tradition: A History of Second Temple and Rabbinic Judaism* (Hoboken, N.J.: Ktav, 1991) 149–56.

4. See the recent survey by J. P. Meier, *A Marginal Jew: Rethinking the Historical Jesus* (New York: Doubleday, 1991) 253–85.

5. A critical review of these polemics is available in J. Neusner, *From Politics to Piety: The Emergence of Pharisaic Judaism* (Englewood Cliffs, N.J.: Prentice-Hall, 1973) 67–80.

6. Babylonian Talmud, *Nedarim* 22a-b.

7. *Midrash Le-Olam* (ed. A. Jellinek, Bet Ha-Midrash 3 [Jerusalem: Wahrmann Books, 1967]) 117.

8. Ethics of the Fathers (Mishnah, ʾAvot) 3:11.

9. Babylonian Talmud, *Bava Metzia* 58b.

10. Cf. S. Lieberman, *Greek in Jewish Palestine* (New York: Phillip Feldheim, 1965) 115–43.

11. Mishnah, *Nedarim* 3:3.

12. Babylonian Talmud, *Nedarim* 77b.

13. L. H. Schiffman, *Sectarian Law in the Dead Sea Scrolls: Courts, Testimony and the Penal Code* (Chico, Calif.: Scholars Press, 1983) 138–39.

14. Some of these are collected in C. G. Montefiore and H. Loewe, *A Rabbinic Anthology* (Philadelphia: Jewish Publication Society, 1963) 460–69.

15. Maimonides, Laws of Repentance 3:10.

16. Laws of Gifts to the Poor 10:8–9.

17. Mishnah, *Shekalim* 5:6; Babylonian Talmud, *Bava Batra* 10a-b.

18. On the widespread character of this statement, see R. C. Collins, "Golden Rule" (*ABD*; New York: Doubleday, 1992), 2: 1070–71.

19. Babylonian Talmud, *Shabbat* 31a.

20. Sifra, *Kedoshim*, 4 (*Sifra de-Ve Rav*, ed. I. H. Weiss [New York: OM Publishing, 1946]) 89b.

21. G. Friedlander, *The Jewish Sources of the Sermon on the Mount* (Hoboken, N.J.: Ktav, 1969) 226–38.

22. This passage appears not to have been preserved in the Qumran fragments. Cf. *Ep. Arist.* 207 for a similar formulation

directed at the king. This text is certainly pre-Christian in its date. See also Ben Sira 31:15, "Judge your neighbor's feelings by your own." Ben Sira dates to c. 180 B.C.E.

23. As quoted by Eusebius, *Praeparatio Evangelica* 8.7.6. Cf. M. Stern, *Greek and Latin Authors on Jews and Judaism II* (Jerusalem: Israel Academy of Sciences and Humanities, 1980) 633.

24. Ethics of the Fathers (Mishnah, 'Avot 2:10).

25. A somewhat later Talmudic approach in cases like this may be worth noting. The rabbis always said that the purpose of creating negative formulations for positive requirements was to add a negative commandment where there already was a positive one, thus making its violation a more severe offense.

26. E. P. Sanders, *Jewish Law from Jesus to the Messiah* (London: SCM Press/Philadelphia: Trinity Press International, 1990) 28.

27. *Genesis Rabbah* 44:1 (ed. J. Theodor, Ch. Albeck [Jerusalem: Wahrmann Books, 1965]) I: 424–25; *Midrash Psalms* 18:25 (ed. S. Buber [Vilna: Romm, 1890–91]) 152.

28. Laws of Forbidden Foods 17:32.

29. E. P. Sanders, "The Life of Jesus," in H. Shanks, ed., *Christianity and Rabbinic Judaism: A Parallel History of Their Origins and Early Development* (Washington, D.C.: Biblical Archaeology Society, 1992) 62–65.

30. Tosefta, *Shabbat* 14 (15):3; Babylonian Talmud, *Shabbat* 128b.

31. *Zadokite Fragments* 11:13-14. Cf. L. H. Schiffman, *The Halakhah at Qumran* (Leiden: Brill, 1975) 121–22.

32. On this process, see L. H. Schiffman, *Who Was a Jew? Rabbinic and Halakhic Perspectives on the Jewish Christian Schism* (Hoboken, N.J.: Ktav, 1985).

CHAPTER 4   JESUS AND THE FIRST TABLE OF THE JEWISH LAW

1. Philo, *Special Laws* 2.63. The two tables are often, here as elsewhere, indicated by such terms as "piety" and "holiness" (both indicating observance of commandments governing relations with

God) and "justice," "righteousness," and "love of humans" (treatment of other people). See E. P. Sanders, *Judaism: Practice and Belief* (Philadelphia: Trinity Press International, 1992) 192–94, and, more fully, "The Question of Uniqueness in the Teaching of Jesus," The Ethel M. Wood Lecture, 1990 (London: University of London, 1990) 28f., n. 26.

2. I have quoted the New Revised Standard Version. For the first clause, the RSV has "The Lord our God is one Lord."

3. Philo, *Special Laws* 1.299f., 324.

4. Tobit 4:15; Philo, *Hypothetica* 7.6; Hillel, according to *Shabbat* 31a.

5. *Sifre Deuteronomy* 54, end. For similar cases and discussion of the logic of this point, see E. P. Sanders, *Paul and Palestinian Judaism* (Philadelphia: Fortress, 1977) 134–38.

6. Matthew 22:34-40 is very similar; see also Luke 10:25-28.

7. *Ep. Aristeas* 234.

8. For a few passages, see Sanders, *Paul and Palestinian Judaism* 107–9 and subject index, under "Intention."

9. See, e.g., Ezek 20:12-24; Neh 10:31; 13:15-22.

10. See 1 Maccabees 2:29-42; Josephus, *J.W.* 1.57-60; 1.145-47; 2.147; *Ant.* 13.252; 14.202; 14.237; *Covenant of Damascus* (*CD*) 10.14–11.18. For discussion of these and other passages, see E. P. Sanders, *Jewish Law from Jesus to the Mishnah* (Philadelphia: Trinity Press International, 1990) 6–8.

11. Sanders, *Jewish Law from Jesus to the Mishnah* 8–14.

12. Josephus, *J.W.* 1.145-47.

13. See *CD* 11.10, accepting the interpretation of *sam* as referring to medicine. See Chaim Rabin, *The Zadokite Documents* (2d ed.; Oxford: Clarendon Press, 1958) 56. For the rabbis, see Mishnah tractate *Shabbat*.

14. Mishnah, *Shabbat* 14.4.

15. Josephus, *Ant.* 14.226, 261. See discussion of this and other rights sought by diaspora Jews in Sanders, *Judaism: Practice and Belief* 211f.

16. Sanders, *Jewish Law from Jesus to the Mishnah* 23–28.

17. See A. B. Du Toit, "Hyperbolical Contrasts: A Neglected Aspect of Paul's Style," *A South African Perspective on the New Testament*, Essays presented to Bruce Manning Metzger (ed. J. H. Petzer and P. J. Martin [Leiden: Brill, 1986]) 178–86; Sanders, *Jewish Law from Jesus to the Mishnah* 28.

18. Acts 10:12 has "all kinds of animals and reptiles and birds of the air"; in Peter's retelling, the phrase is "animals and beasts of prey and reptiles and birds of the air" (Acts 11:6).

19. Circumcision: Gal 2:3 and elsewhere; food: perhaps Gal 2:11-13; Sabbath: Gal 4:10.

20. Sanders, *Jewish Law from Jesus to the Mishnah* part I.

21. Handwashing: ibid., 260–63, and further pages listed in the index.

22. Sanders, *Jesus and Judaism* (Philadelphia: Fortress, 1985) 296–301; *Jewish Law from Jesus to the Mishnah* 57–67; *The Historical Figure of Jesus* (London: Penguin, 1993) 270–73.

CHAPTER 5   FROM JESUS TO CHRIST: THE CONTRIBUTION OF THE APOSTLE PAUL

1. "At the present time [that is, by midcentury] there is a remnant [of Israel] chosen by grace" (Rom 11:5); only the elect of Israel, such as Paul, believe the gospel, and the rest are hardened (Rom 11:7). At what point did Gentiles enter the Jesus movement? During his lifetime, Jesus himself seems to have preached primarily to his fellow Jews, and certain passages in the later gospels reflect this (e.g., Mark 7:24-30, the Syrophoenician women, cf. Matt. 15:24; Matt. 10:6, 23). Acts 11:19 suggests that later apostles preserved this policy until quite late. But significant numbers of Gentiles lived in territorial Israel in the first century, and there is little reason to think that Gentiles would have joined only after the movement went out into the Diaspora.

2. Scholarly consensus holds that Mark was written c. 70 C.E., Matthew, Luke, and John some twenty years after that, and the book of Acts—Part II of Luke's Gospel—c. 90–100 C.E. The Gospels are

166

originally anonymous, and the names we know them by were assigned by various Christian communities only in the mid-second century. Although their respective writers base their stories in part on traditions that might ultimately go back to the circle originally around Jesus, they do not themselves count as primary evidence in the way that Paul does.

3. The other letters—Ephesians, Colossians, 2 Thessalonians, 1 and 2 Timothy, and Titus—are considered *deutero-Pauline*, that is, written by later Christians who looked to Paul for their inspiration and authority. The Pauline authorship of Hebrews has been disputed since antiquity.

4. Paul preserves only a description of the Parousia (Jesus' Second Coming), similar to the evangelical Son of man traditions, as a saying ("This we declare to you by the word of the Lord") in 1 Thessalonians 4:15-18; a saying prohibiting divorce (1 Cor. 7:10-11); and the eucharistic formula (1 Cor 11:23-26).

5. E.g., his closing statement in Romans, his final letter, where he speaks of the (gentile) Christian community as proof of God's scripturally attested constancy toward Israel, 15:8-9.

6. Paul sees himself as the apostle to the Gentiles par excellence; but it is clear from his own letter to the Romans that other *apostoloi* had established the community there: Paul writes ahead to introduce himself in advance of his arrival (Rom 1:8-15; 15:20-22).

7. Cf. the similar lists of vices: Gal 5:19-21 (these characterized simply as "the works of the flesh"); Rom 13:12-13; 1 Cor 6:9-11 (personal, not abstract nouns: "idolators, adulterers, sexual perverts. . . . And such were some of you"). For discussions of such lists in other Hellenistic Jewish authors, see E. Käsemann, *Commentary on Romans* (Grand Rapids: Eerdmans, 1980) 49f.

8. See esp. E. P. Sanders, "Jewish Association with Gentiles and Galatians 2:11-14," in *Studies in Paul and John in honor of J. Louis Martyn* (Nashville: Abingdon, 1990) 170-89.

9. Traditional Mediterranean cults were, first of all, local (associated with particular sites and cities) and, second, nonexclusive: one could worship the gods of a particular locality as well as join whatever specific cults (e.g., to Isis, or Serapis) one chose, with no

conflict. Only Judaism and, eventually, Christianity forbade multiple religious associations for full members. For a dated but still valuable discussion of this aspect of pagan religious sensibility, see A. D. Nock, *Conversion* (New York: Clarendon Press, 1933); more recently, Robin Lane Fox, *Pagans and Christians* (New York: Knopf, 1987).

10. *de vita Moysis* 2.41.

11. For example, the anonymous pagan author of the Paris Magical Papyrus (third century C.E.) instructs would-be exorcists to adjure demons "by the god of the Hebrews . . . say, 'I adjure thee by him who appeared to Osrael in a pillar of light and the cloud by day . . . I adjure thee by the seal which Solomon laid upon the tongue of Jeremiah . . . .'" This charm may have been copied from a Jewish magical handbook, but the confusions in biblical chronology incline me to suspect that our magician relied on impressions from memory. For the full English text of this particular charm, see C. K. Barrett, *The New Testament Background* (New York: Macmillan, 1961) 31–35; for the corpus, H. D. Betz, *Greek Magical Papyri in Translation* (Chicago: University of Chicago Press, 1986) vol. 1.

12. Josephus, *J.W.* 2.18.2 (they can be found in every city in Syria); *J.W.* 7.7.3 (Greeks attend synagogue services in Antioch and after their fashion become part of the community). See Fergus Millar's review of the evidence in E. Schürer, G. Vermes et al., *The History of the Jewish People in the Age of Jesus Christ* (175 B.C.–A.D. 135) (4 vols.; Edinburgh: T. & T. Clark, 1973–87) 3:166ff. Such Gentiles turn up routinely in Luke's synagogues (Acts 10:2, 22; 13:16, 26, 43, 50; 16:14, 17:4, 17; 18:7.

13. Horace, *Satires* 1.4.142-3; Juvenal, *Satires* 14.96-106. For an extensive collection of material, see Menachem Stern, *Greek and Latin Authors on Jews and Judaism* (3 vol.; Jerusalem: Israel Academy 1974–84).

14. This inscription is translated and analyzed by Joyce Reynolds and Robert Tannenbaum, *Jews and Godfearers at Aphrodisias* (Cambridge: Cambridge University Press, 1987); see also P. Fredriksen, "Judaism, the Circumcision of Gentiles, and Apocalyptic Hope: Another Look at Galatians 1 and 2," *JTSNS* 42 (1991) 532–64, esp. 541ff.

15. Tertulliian, *ad Nationes* 1.13.3-4 (some pagans keep Sabbath and Passover, but still worship at traditional altars too); Cyril of Alexandria, *de adoratione in spiritu et veritate* 3.92.3 (men in Phoenicia and Palestine, calling themselves Godfearers, follow consistently neither Jewish nor Greek custom); Commodian, *Instructiones* 37.1 (some people live between both ways, rushing between synagogue and shrine). For further primary evidence, see Fredriksen, "Judaism, the Circumcision of Gentiles, and Apocalyptic Hope" 543 and nn 34–35.

16. Humanity begins twice in Genesis, once with Adam and Eve, and later (Gen 6–9) with Noah and his family. Rabbinic tradition eventually teased from Gen. 9:1-7 seven rules of moral behavior encumbent on all Gentiles, the so-called Noachite Commandments, which prohibit idolatry, blasphemy, fornication, violent bloodshed, theft, and eating the flesh from a living animal, and enjoin the formation of courts of law. For a comprehensive discussion, see David Novak, *The Image of the Non-Jew in Judaism* (Toronto: Edwin Mellen Press, 1983). James's ruling in Acts 15:20 may provide a first-century witness to this tradition; cf. Jubilees 7:20ff.; Avodah Zarah 8(9):4-6.

17. A central prayer in the synagogue service, also known as the *Shemoneh Esreh* or Eighteen Benedictions. I quote from the Orthodox Prayer Service, *ha-Siddur ha-Shalem* (trans. Philip Birnbaum [New York: San Ledrin Press, 1977]): "Blessed are You, Lord our God and God of our fathers . . . who are Master of all things; . . . who will graciously bring a redeemer . . . ; You are mighty forever; You revive the dead with great mercy, and support the living with kindness. . . . You bring death and restore life, and cause salvation to flourish. . . . Redeem us speedily for your name's sake, for you are a mighty Redeemer. Blessed are you, O Lord, Redeemer of Israel. . . . Sound the great shofar of our freedom; lift up the banner to bring our exiles together; assemble us from the four corners of the earth. . . . Return in mercy to your city Jerusalem and dwell in it . . . ; rebuild it soon, in our days . . . speedily cause the offspring of your servant David to flourish. . . . Blessed are you, O Lord, who hears prayer."

18. "We hope therefore, Lord our God, soon to behold your majestic glory . . . when the world shall be perfected under the reign of the Almighty . . . ."

19. Traditionally, the prophecy of Daniel is joined with the other classical prophecies; historically, its period of composition is much later, in the time of the Maccabean Revolt.

20. For an introductory discussion, see P. Fredriksen, *From Jesus to Christ* (New Haven: Yale University Press, 1988) 70–93.

21. "There will be wars and rumors of wars. . . . Nation with rise against nation, and kingdom against kingdom. There will be earthquakes in various places; there will be famines. . . . In those days there will be such tribulation as has not been from the beginning of the Creation until now. . . . The sun will be darkened, the moon will not give its light; the stars will be falling from heaven, and the powers of the heavens will be shaken. . . . Truly, this generation will not pass away before all these things take place" (Mark 13:7-30, a fairly typical catalog of disasters).

22. Again, these ancient apocalyptic hopes are canonized in the daily prayer service. I quote the second paragraph of the *Alenu*: "We hope, therefore, Lord our God, soon to behold your majestic glory, *when the abominations shall be removed from the earth and the false gods exterminated*; when the world shall be perfected under the reign of the Almighty, and all humankind [in Hebrew, *kol benei basar*] will call upon your name, and *all the wicked of the earth will be turned to you*. May all the inhabitants of the world realize that to you every knee must bend, every tongue vow allegiance . . . and give honor to your glorious name." This is close to Paul's language in Philippians 2:9-11: "Therefore God has highly exalted him [Jesus] and bestowed upon him the name which is above every name, that at the name of Jesus every knee should bow . . . and every tongue confess that Jesus is Lord, to the glory of God the Father."

23. E.g., 1 Corinthians: a warning against fraternizing with a Christian Gentile "if he is guilty of immorality or greed, or is an idolator" (5:11); "Do not worship idols" (10:7); "Shun the worship of idols" (10:14); "They sacrifice to demons, not to God. I do not

want you to be partners with demons. You cannot drink the cup of the Lord and the cup of demons" (10:20-21).

24. Circumcision was considered the sign of (male) conversion to Judaism universally, i.e., by Jewish, pagan, and, later, Christian observers. For citations to various primary sources, see Fredriksen, "Judaism, the Circumcision of Gentiles, and Apocalyptic Hope" 536 and nn 11–12.

25. Judaism was a religion of conversion—ways existed for volunteers to join—but never a religion of missions. See Fredriksen, ibid.; also, Scot McKnight, *A Light among the Gentiles* (Minneapolis: Fortress, 1991), although he confuses the Gentiles' Endtime inclusion with actual conversion.

26. Philippians: the day of Jesus Christ (1:6); the day of Christ (1:10); the day of Christ (2:16); we await our Savior the Lord Jesus Christ (3:20).

27. E.g., Dan 12:2-3; 2 Macc 7 (the martyrdom of the seven brothers).

28. "If the spirit of Him who raised Jesus from the dead dwells in you, he who raised Christ Jesus from the dead will give life to your mortal bodies also through His spirit which dwells in you" (Rom 8:11); "Christ has been raised, the first fruits of those who have fallen asleep. . . . For as in Adam all die, so also in Christ shall all be made alive. But each in his own order: Christ the first fruits; then at his coming those who belong to Christ. Then comes the End, when he delivers the Kingdom to God the Father" (1 Cor 15:20-24).

29. E.g., the itinerary of the new movement implied in Galatians 1; the Risen Christ's mission charge at the end of the Gospel of Matthew (Matt 28); the Risen Christ's charge in Acts 1:8: "You shall be my witnesses in Jerusalem and in all Judea and Samaria and to the ends of the earth."

30. For my reconstruction of Jesus' views on God's Kingdom, see Fredriksen, *From Jesus to Christ* 94–130.

31. We see Paul already enunciate this interpolation in Romans 9–11, where Christ seems to wait on Paul's achieving the "full number" of Gentiles before coming back. In the Synoptic Gospels,

Jesus announces that the space between his resurrection and return should be filled with missionary activity (e.g., Mark 13:10 and passim; cf. Matt 10:16-23), and the Risen Christ makes this explicit (Matt 28:19-20; cf. Luke 24:46-48; Acts 1:8). In the late first/early second century, the author of 2 Peter admitted that the time between the resurrection and Parousia was stretching on, but counseled that God was giving to as many people as possible more time to repent before the End (2 Pt 3:9), and that these very doubts about the End were proof that it was nigh (2 Pt 3).

CHAPTER 6   FROM CRUCIFIED MESSIAH TO RISEN CHRIST: THE TRIAL OF JESUS REVISITED

1. All biblical citations and translations, unless otherwise noted, are from the *New Revised Standard Version*.

2. Gerald S. Sloyan, *Jesus on Trial: The Development of the Passion Narratives and Their Historical and Ecumenical Implications* (Philadelphia: Fortress Press, 1973) viii.

3. The most comprehensive treatment of the issues involved is found in Raymond E. Brown, *The Death of the Messiah: From Gethsemane to the Grave, A Commentary on the Passion Narratives in the Four Gospels* (2 vols.; New York: Doubleday, 1994). Brown's extensive treatment (more than 1,600 pages) of all aspects of the passion narrative will set the agenda for years to come. His discussion of the "Jewish Trial" (315–660, 1418–34) is itself a virtual monograph complete with extensive bibliographies (315–27, 563–67). Unfortunately, I received his work only in the final stages of editing this essay, and although I draw on it selectively, I do not claim to offer an adequate appropriation of his work. (Although this is a two-volume work, the pages are numbered sequentially, so I will refer simply to page numbers rather than volume and page.) Some other important recent studies on the trial of Jesus are the essays collected in Ernst Bammel, ed., *The Trial of Jesus: Cambridge Essays in Honour of C. F. D. Moule* (SBT 13; London: SCM Press, 1970); Ernst Bammel and C. F. D. Moule, eds., *Jesus and the Politics of His Day* (Cambridge:

Cambridge University Press, 1984); Frank J. Matera, "The Trial of Jesus: Problems and Proposals," *Int* 45 (1991) 5–16; Fergus Millar, "Reflections on the Trial of Jesus," in P. R. Davies and R. T. White, eds., *A Tribute to Geza Vermes: Essays on Jewish and Christian Literature and History* (JSOTSup 100; Sheffield: JSOT Press, 1990) 354–81.

4. John R. Donahue, *Are You the Christ? The Trial Narrative in the Gospel of Mark* (SBLDS 10; Missoula: Society of Biblical Literature, 1973), and "Temple, Trial and Royal Christology (Mark 14:53-65)," in Werner H. Kelber, ed., *The Passion in Mark: Studies on Mark 14–16* (Philadelphia: Fortress, 1976) 61–79.

5. Donahue, *Trial* 238–39.

6. An excellent survey is found in David R. Catchpole, *The Trial of Jesus: A Study in the Gospels and Jewish Historiography from 1770 to the Present Time* (SPB 18; Leiden: Brill, 1971), and "The Problem of the Historicity of the Sanhedrin Trial," in Bammel, ed., *The Trial of Jesus* 47–65. Very influential in the discussion were the extensive writings of P. J. Winter (listed in Catchpole, *Trial* 294), culminating in Winter, *On the Trial of Jesus* (SJ 1; Berlin: Walter de Gruyter, 1961).

7. Donald Juel, *Messiah and Temple: The Trial of Jesus in the Gospel of Mark* (SBLDS 31; Missoula: Scholars Press, 1977).

8. Ibid. 211.

9. Sloyan, note 2 above.

10. Ibid. 134.

11. Despite the immense amount of historical knowledge that informs his work, Raymond Brown adopts a redaction critical approach and states as his fundamental purpose, "to explain in detail what the evangelists intended and conveyed to their audiences by their narratives of the passion and death of Jesus" (*Death* 4).

12. Brown, *Death*; Martin Goodman, *The Ruling Class of Judaea: The Origins of the Jewish Revolt against Rome A.D. 66–70* (Cambridge: Cambridge University Press, 1987); James S. McLaren, *Power and Politics in Palestine: The Jews and the Governing of their Land 100 B.C.–A.D. 70* (JSNTSup 63; Sheffield: JSOT Press, 1991); E. P. Sanders, *Judaism: Practice and Belief 63 B.C.E.–66 C.E.* (Philadelphia: Trinity Press International, 1992).

13. "Sanhedrin," *IDB* 4.214; similarly, F. F. Bruce calls the Sanhedrin "their [i.e., the Jewish people's] senate and supreme court": see "Palestine, Administration of (Roman)" *ABD* (New York: Doubleday, 1992) 5.98.

14. Sanders, *Judaism* 471.

15. Ibid. 458.

16. McLaren, *Power* 213.

17. Ibid.

18. For a summary of the discrepancies between the gospel accounts and the later Mishnaic procedures, see Brown, *Death* 358–59. Sadly, these procedures in the Mishnah have often been used in an anti-Semitic fashion to enhance the malice of first-century Jewish leaders who were thought to be violating their own laws.

19. Along with Sanders, *Judaism*, see esp. Joseph A. Fitzmyer, "From Pompey to Bar Kochba" (*NJBC*; Englewood Cliffs, N.J.: Prentice-Hall, 1990) 1243–52; E. Schürer, G. Vermes, et al., *The History of the Jewish People in the Age of Jesus Christ (175 B.C.–A.D. 135)* (4 vols; Edinburgh: T. & T. Clark, 1973–87) vols. 1–2; E. Mary Smallwood, *The Jews under Roman Rule: From Pompey to Diocletian* (SJLA 20; Leiden: Brill, 1976).

20. Schürer, *History* 1:320–35; Fitzmyer, "From Pompey" 1247.

21. Josephus, *J.W.* 1.648-55; *Ant.* 17.149-67. All references to Josephus are from Josephus, Loeb Classical Library (10 vols.; Cambridge: Harvard University Press, 1926–65).

22. Fitzmyer, "From Pompey" 1248.

23. Richard A. Horsley, with John S. Hanson, *Bandits, Prophets and Messiahs: Popular Movements at the Time of Jesus* (San Francisco: Harper & Row, 1985) 111.

24. *Ant.* 17.295.

25. David Rhoads, "Zealots" *ABD* 6:1043–52. Rhoads (1046) attributes this view principally to S. G. F. Brandon, *Jesus and the Zealots* (New York: Scribner's, 1967), and Martin Hengel, esp. *Victory over Violence: Jesus and the Revolutionaries* (Philadelphia: Fortress, 1975). An early criticism of this view is M. Smith, "Zealots and Sicarii: Their Origins and Relations," *HTR* 64 (1971) 1–19. In

numerous important studies, Richard Horsley has rendered such a view obsolete, while simultaneously depicting the diverse forms of social unrest in the first century C.E.; see esp. *Bandits, Prophets, and Jesus and the Spiral of Violence* (San Francisco: Harper & Row, 1987); "Popular Messianic Movements around the Time of Jesus," *CBQ* 46 (1984) 471–95; "The Zealots: Their Origin, Relationships and Importance in the Jewish Revolt," *NovT* 27 (1986) 159–92. Zealots should be reserved for a separate group that emerges only in the latter stages of the Jewish War of 66–70 C.E.

26. Horsley, *Bandits* 197.

27. Goodman, *Ruling Class* 95.

28. On Josephus as an apologist, see Gregory E. Sterling, *Historiography and Self-definition: Josephos, Luke–Acts and Apologetic Historiography* (NovTSup 64; Leiden: Brill, 1992) esp. 308–10.

29. Brown, *Death* 677–79.

30. Fitzmyer ("From Pompey" 1246) gives a list of the high priests from 37 B.C.E. to 67 C.E., along with those who appointed them. See also Goodman, *Ruling Class* 109–11.

31. Brown (*Death* 336–37) notes that, until quite recently, Pilate was called "procurator" (see Josephus, *J.W.* 2.169). Recent research, which Brown summarizes well, shows that "prefect" is the more proper term. See also the inscription found in Caesarea in 1961 where Pilate is called the "[Praef]ectus Juda[ea]e" (ibid. 695).

32. Goodman (*Ruling Class* 143) calls attention to the power of the five sons of Ananus, and agrees that Caiaphas is son-in-law of Annas.

33. Goodman, *Ruling Class* 29.

34. A. N. Sherwin-White, *Roman Society and Roman Law in the New Testament* (Oxford: Clarendon Press, 1963) 3.

35. McLaren (*Power* 188–93) emphasizes strongly that the normal mode of dealing with difficult issues was negotiation rather than confrontation.

36. Sanders, *Judaism* 323.

37. Zvi Greenhut, "Burial Grave of the Caiaphas Family," *BAR* 18 (1992) 35.

38. Sanders, *Judaism* 493.

39. See the important essays of Dahl, collected in *Jesus the Christ: The Historical Origins of Christological Doctrine* (Minneapolis: Fortress, 1991); also, "Messianic Ideas and the Crucifixion of Jesus," in James H. Charlesworth, ed., *The Messiah: Developments in Earliest Judaism and Christianity* (Minneapolis: Fortress, 1992) 382–403; and Donald Juel, *Messianic Exegesis: Christological Interpretation of the Old Testament in Early Christianity* (Minneapolis: Fortress, 1988).

40. Matt. 27:37; Mark 15:26; Luke 23:38; John 19:19.) Bammel notes that, although the *titulus* is a solid bit of evidence, it should be taken in conjunction with other evidence—principally, the trial. See "The *titulus*," in Bammel and Moule, eds., *Jesus and the Politics* 364.

41. Gerald G. O'Collins, "Crucifixion," *ABD* 1:1207–10.

42. Brown, *Death* 472–80, esp. 475.

43. Ibid. 480.

44. William Wrede, *The Messianic Secret* (Cambridge/London: James Clark, 1971). Germ orig. 1901.

45. *The Gospel according to Luke I–IX*, AB 28A (Garden City: Doubleday, 1981) 198. See also Brown, *Death* 474–75 ". . . although Josephus describes all sorts of historical figures (prophets, would-be kings, priests, agitators) in the 1st cent. A.D., he never calls one of them a Messiah."

46. Zwi Werblowsky, "Jewish Messianism in Comparative Perspective," in Ithamar Gruenwald, Shaul Shaked, and Gedaliahu Strousma, eds. *Messiah and Christos: Studies in the Jewish Origins of Christianity* (Tübingen: J. C. B. Mohr [Paul Siebeck], 1992) 1.

47. Ibid. 2.

48. Charlesworth, *The Messiah*.

49. Ibid. 11.

50. Ibid. 35.

51. Brown, among others, calls attention to Josephus's account of Jesus bar Ananias in c. 62 C.E. (*War* 6.300-309) and its importance for understanding social and legal issues surrounding the death of Jesus. Jesus bar Ananias, "a rude peasant" began to cry out constantly against the temple. Some "leading citizens" arrested and

chastised him (6.302), but he continued his cries. Then the magistrates (*archontes*) brought him to the Roman governor, Albinus, who dismissed him as a maniac. Jesus continued his shouting for "seven years and five months" until he was killed by a *balista* during the siege of Jerusalem. This case shows that not every disturbance in Jerusalem or every "attack" on the temple merited crucifixion. Also, according to Brown (*Death* 715), it shows that Roman governors retained a certain independence in the face of accusation from Jewish officials.

52. Jerome Murphy-O'Connor, "John the Baptist and Jesus: History and Hypothesis," *NTS* 36 (1990) 359–74.

53. For recent interpretations of the work of John, see Paul Hollenbach, "Social Aspects of John the Baptizer's Preaching Mission in the Context of Palestinian Judaism," *ANRW* II/19/1 (1979) 850–75; and "John the Baptist," *ABD* 3:887–99.

54. On development of traditions of John the Baptist, see W. Wink, *John the Baptist in the Gospel Tradition* (SNTSMS 7; Cambridge: Cambridge University Press, 1968).

55. E. P. Sanders, *Jesus and Judaism* (Philadelphia: Fortress, 1985) 61–76.

56. "Jesus and the Temple, Mark and the War," in SBLSP 29 (ed. D. J. Lull [Atlanta: Scholars Press, 1990]) 290.

57. Craig Evans, "Jesus' Action in the Temple: Cleansing or Portent of Destruction?," *CBQ* 51 (1989) 237–69.

58. See V. Eppstein, "The Historicity of the Cleansing of the Temple," *ZNW* 55 (1964) 42–58, cited in Evans, "Jesus' Action" 265.

59. I have used "handing over" rather than betrayal. The technical term used throughout for Judas' action is *paradidonai* rather than *prodidonai*, which is the technical term for betrayal (see Luke 6:16, where Judas is called *prodotēs*), following Brown (*Death* 1399), who also suggests that the use of *paradidonai* may be due to the influence of Isa 53:12 (LXX).

60. See William Klassen, "Judas," *ABD* 3:1091–96.

61. Millar, "Reflections"; Smallwood, *The Jews,* 172.

62. Smallwood, *The Jews,* 172.

63. Ibid. 279.

64. Brown (*Death* 336–38) favors the view of those Roman historians who hold that the governor had virtually unlimited power to execute in a case such as that of Jesus.

65. The literature on Jesus' kingdom proclamation is vast. A remarkable fact of contemporary scholarship is that, amid the avalanche of conflicting reconstructions of the historical Jesus, virtually everyone admits that his kingdom proclamation is at the bedrock of his ministry. The connection between the kingdom proclamation and the death of Jesus is explored briefly by Brown (*Death* 478–89) and more extensively in an important article by Craig Evans, "From Public Ministry to Passion: Can a Link Be Found between the (Galilean) Life and the (Judaean) Death of Jesus?," in SBLSP 32 (ed. Eugene Lovering [Atlanta: Scholars Press, 1993]) 460–72.

66. Dennis C. Duling, "Solomon, Exorcism and the Son of David, *HTR* 68 (1975) 236–52; see also his other studies on Davidic motifs in the New Testament, "The Promises to David and Their Entrance into Christianity—Nailing Down a Likely Hypothesis," *NTS* 20 (1973) 55–77, and "The Therapeutic Son of David: An Element in Matthew's Christological Apologetic," *NTS* 24 (1977) 392–410.

67. Evans, "From Public Ministry" 466.

68. J. P. Meier, *A Marginal Jew: Rethinking the Historical Jesus* (New York: Doubleday, 1991) 350; see also 207, 277.

69. John Dominic Crossan, *The Historical Jesus: The Life of a Mediterranean Jewish Peasant* (San Francisco: HarperSanFrancisco, 1992) 452.

70. See text and discussion in Meier, *A Marginal Jew* 96. After surveying all the evidence in antiquity of action against Jesus by Jewish authorities, Brown (*Death* 377) states: "Nevertheless, whether we appeal to direct or indirect evidence, there is no ancient indication of any Jewish tradition that calls into doubt the involvement of Jewish authorities in the death of Jesus."

71. Ibid. 391–97.

72. Id. 393.

73. Id. 394; Joseph A. Fitzmyer, *Responses to 101 Questions on the Dead Sea Scrolls* (New York: Paulist Press, 1992) 57–58. After

careful study of the texts pertinent to the issue of the execution of the Teacher of Righteousness, Fitzmyer concludes that it is "not impossible."

74. Brown, *Death* 396.

75. Ibid.

76. Charlesworth, "From Messianology to Christology," in *The Messiah* 33–34.

77. Juel, *Messianic Exegesis* 59–88.

78. Ibid. and 99–110.

79. P. Fredriksen, *From Jesus to Christ* (New Haven: Yale University Press, 1988) 133.

80. Ibid. 134.

81. See the helpful summary in Peter Hodgson, *Jesus Word and Presence* (Philadelphia: Fortress, 1971) 246–50.

82. Barnabas Lindars, *New Testament Apologetic: The Doctrinal Significance of Old Testament Quotations* (Philadelphia: Westminster, 1961) 32–51.

83. See Crossan, *The Historical Jesus*.

84. See Burton Mack, *A Myth of Innocence: Mark and Christian Origins* (Philadelphia: Fortress, 1988), and *The Lost Gospel: The Book of Q and Christian Origins* (San Francisco: HarperSanFrancisco, 1991) 203: "If we ask about the speaker of this kind of material, it has its nearest analogy in contemporary profiles of the Cynic-sage. This is as close to the historical Jesus as Q allows us to get."

85. "Should Christmas Mean Anything to Jews," in Daniel C. Matt, ed., *Walking Humbly With God: The Life and Writings of Rabbi Hershel Jonah Matt* (Hoboken, N.J.: Ktav, 1993) 212. I owe this reference to Daniel Matt, a colleague at the Graduate Theological Union.

CHAPTER 7   OUTLINING THE QUESTION: FROM CHRIST TO GOD

1. Donald Juel, *Messianic Exegesis: Christological Interpretations of the Old Testament in Early Christianity* (Minneapolis: Fortress, 1988).

2. Nils A. Dahl, *The Crucified Messiah and Other Essays* (Minneapolis: Augsburg, 1974).

3. James H. Charlesworth ed., *Old Testament Pseudepigrapha* (2 vols.; Garden City: Doubleday, 1983, 1985).

4. See James H. Charlesworth, *Jesus and the Dead Sea Scrolls* (New York: Doubleday, 1992). For a thorough treatment of the notion of messiah, see James H. Charlesworth ed., *The Messiah: Developments in Earliest Judaism and Christianity* (Minneapolis: Fortress, 1992).

5. Larry W. Hurtado, *One God, One Lord: Early Christian Devotion and Ancient Jewish Monotheism* (Philadelphia: Fortress, 1988). See also Alan F. Segal, *Rebecca's Children: Judaism and Christianity in the Roman World* (Cambridge: Harvard University Press, 1986) and *Paul the Convert: The Apostolate and Apostasy of Saul of Tarsus* (New Haven: Yale University Press, 1990).

CHAPTER 8   FROM CHRIST TO GOD: THE CHRISTIAN PERSPECTIVE

1. Acts 2:36. This and subsequent biblical quotations are taken from the New Revised Standard Version.

2. *Letters of Ignatius of Antioch*: Romans 1. Translation of this sentence taken from Henry Bettenson, *The Early Christian Fathers* (London: Oxford University Press, 1956).

3. Athenagoras, *Plea for Christians* (trans. J. H. Crehan [New York: Newman, 1956]) ch. 10.1ff.

4. Origen, *On First Principles* (trans. G. W. Butterworth [New York: Harper Torch Books, 1967]).

5. It is difficult to illustrate these perceptions of Hippolytus and Tertullian in single quotations. The cumulative evidence of how these two authors understood the divinity of Jesus in relation to their concepts of God has been traced in some detail by J. N. D. Kelly, *Early Christian Doctrines* (2d ed.; New York: Harper & Row, 1960) ch. VI.

6. The relevant texts are to be found in the original language in the *Enchiridion Symbolorum* of Denzinger-Schoenmetzer but

appear in translation in many collections. A particularly helpful version is in Edward R. Hardy, ed., *Christology of the Later Fathers* (Philadelphia: Westminster, 1955). Documents 371–74.

7. A helpful selection of these is also to be found in Hardy, ibid.

8. This was most explicitly expressed in Anselm's *Cur Deus homo* and has continued to be very influential in Christian piety.

9. I have made this case at greater length in M. K. Hellwig, *Jesus, the Compassion of God* (Collegeville, Minn.: Liturgical Press/ Glazier, 1983).

Subject Index

SCRIPTURE INDEX